MEDIA

DIGITAL

RANTS

POSTPOLITICS IN THE

NATION

JON KATZ

HARDWIRED

San Francisco

HardWired
520 Third Street, Fourth Floor
San Francisco, CA 94107

First Edition 1997
Printed in the United States of America
10 9 8 7 6 5 4 3 2 1

Library of Congress Cataloging-in-Publication Data

Katz, Jon.
Media Rants : postpolitics in the digital nation / Jon Katz. – 1st ed.
p. cm.
ISBN 1-888869-12-7
1. Mass media and technology–United States. 2. Mass media–
Political aspects–United States. 3. Discourse analysis–Social
aspects–United States. 4. Internet (Computer network) 5. World
Wide Web (Information retrieval system) 6. United States–Politics
and government–1993-   7. Katz, Jon. I. Title.
P96.T422U635   1997
302.23'0973–dc21   97-10195

Design direction and cover design by Susanna Dulkinys
Text design by Pete Friedrich

Typography
Interstate designed by Tobias Frere-Jones (1993)

This book is dedicated to David Weir, Cate Corcoran, Benedict Cosgrove, Kevin Lyons, Anna McMillan and the engineers, researchers, producers, and readers of The Netizen.

NOTE FROM THE EDITOR

When HotWired, Wired's online network, launched The
Netizen in January 1996, many an American with a modem
speculated that 1996 would be the Year of the Net in Politics.
Through daily dispatches, The Netizen intended to record
not just the presidential campaign, but also the hackneyed
habits of old media and the red-hot issues posed by an
economy transformed through electronic communications.
The Web site would question the very relevance of old-
style politics.

Of the several journalists enlisted to write for the Web site,
Jon Katz was charged with critiquing the campaign press,
chronicling the clashes between old media and new ways,
and documenting the emergence of a Digital Nation.

Threads, the online posting area associated with The Netizen,
was conceived as a companion to the site's bylined columns;
it would be a forum in which netizens could debate the
sense and nonsense of the political theater.

The focus of The Netizen evolved; by the time the election
was over it had grown into a vibrant town hall where people
were hashing out social, ethical, and intellectual issues.
The Netizen's tagline changed—from "no politics as usual"
to "the Digital Nation's town hall."

Katz's role, too, evolved. In early '96, he was merely hosting
Threads. But Katz couldn't stop himself. The verbal gunfire
drew him in. What were originally intended to be salvos
that stimulated debate soon expanded. Before long, Katz's
posts were reformatted—given space, headlines, graphics.
They became The Netizen's most popular columns and
carried a new moniker: Media Rants.

In a way, "Media Rants" is a misleading characterization of
Jon Katz's work. For Katz is really **not** a ranter. He is not
an angry man. He may be rash, but he's certainly not rigid.
You might consider Katz a cartoonist who happens to use

nouns and verbs (and, well, lots of adjectives) instead of pen and ink.

But what culture is he lampooning? For Katz, as for many of his readers, media **is** politics **is** pop culture. His column became a magnet for a mash of issues—the travails of The Imperial Press, the untimely death of Tupac Shakur, the dizzying visions of Walt Disney, the many missteps of Bill Gates's Microsoft, the meeting of pop culture and morality.

Katz is so prolific that he has managed to connect with his audience in an unprecedented way: he follows each column with vigorous posts in Threads and extended email dialogues. What sets Katz apart from columnists in **any** media is how much he cares about interacting with readers.

The growth of the Web during the time Katz has been writing on The Netizen has been phenomenal. The year of columns collected here are a barometer of that change. By fall '96, when he took on the likes of NBC and Wal-Mart, Katz became an online version of Larry King or Phil Donahue: he became the orchestrator of electronic "yak-a-thons" who maintains an increasingly intimate relationship with his audience.

Above everything else, Jon Katz champions this interactivity—**the** distinguishing characteristic of the Net. But not everyone has so readily embraced it. Katz is fond of saying that those who fear interactivity the most are journalists and intellectuals. If the **thoughtless** response to the Web is to lambaste its pornography, he argues, the **thoughtful** response is to lambaste its interactivity. Why? Because these thinkers fear losing control of "their" ideas.

At Katz's request, we've made this book interactive by inviting one of Katz's favorite thinkers to respond to his ideas, in an afterword. If Katz is the Web provocateur who takes on Washington and the media elite, Wendy Kaminer is the no-nonsense critic who takes on the Web provocateur.

Constance Hale
San Francisco

POSTP

POST

P

THE INTERACTIVE COLUMNIST

MY YEAR ON THE WEB

Call it my experiment in journalism. The Netizen's content and style often puzzle mainstream-press types. Its layout can confound newcomers to the Net. And my role on the Web does not conform to traditional notions of what a columnist or commentator is.

I've written in the past for newspapers like **The Boston Globe** and **The Philadelphia Inquirer,** and magazines like **Rolling Stone** and **New York.** Writing a Web column has not merely marked a new twist in my writing; it has been a new experience altogether.

Columnists on the Web get the first word but never the last. We are just sparks. Unlike a Washington pundit or op-ed columnist, a critic here doesn't write from a position of authority but in full view of thousands of people who often know more about the subject than the writer and who instantly—and publicly—file corrections, disagreements, and concerns. As on many Web sites, HotWired's Threads (the public posting forum) and a tradition of emails between writer and reader boost its interactive component and instantly challenge the columnist's point of view. "Mass" media brook no such role for the masses—the print or TV columnist may get pestered by a few voicemails or letters to the editor but is mostly free to hit and run.

Suck recently described The Netizen as the digital equivalent of a talk show, but there are important differences. A TV talk show is bounded by visual imagery; talk radio depends on tension and confrontation. This new form is, so far, confined by neither and has a much greater reach.

Columnists on the Web are just getting started when their work is published. Because their work is continually challenged, criticized, and commented upon, columnists here—at least this one—come to view their own opinions differently. Not at all declarations, ideas and notions are almost living editorial organisms.

They evolve, grow, shrink, or change as they radiate from the site, sometimes all over the world, and are constantly returned, often with new ideas or improvements. Columns are discussed, debated, recycled for months after they appear, bouncing back and forth like rubber balls. Every time they come back, it's with a different idea or answer. The idea changes and evolves. Then there are the times an idea sinks under its own ridiculous weight.

This makes the experience feel not so much like a news-paper column or a talk show as a hive — with columns sailing *ruche* **out from the center like digital bees across the Net.**

There is almost nothing I write that I wouldn't write differently just a few weeks later, given the sometimes astonishing variety of feedback. *(réac 0)*

coucher sur le papier

I used to believe everything I committed to paper was right. I'm no longer certain about that — a column is just my best feeling at the time, the beginning of a discussion. There is no better tonic for a writer's arrogance than interactivity. *louange* Praise tends to come in private email, if it comes at all. *déterminé* In fact, the point of Threads is to provide a forum for *la base* criticism and disagreement, not for affirmation or support. This can be unnerving, but it divides old and new media. *déconcertant* The relationship between writer and reader has been altered: the columnist has less power, the reader more. *||*

Threads makes it clear that the columnist is as likely *(plausible)* to be wrong as right, that different opinions and inter-pretations abound, and that the columnist presents just *abonder* one valid point of view. In fact, the willingness to live with *valeur* being wrong (and to have it pointed out ad infinitum) is a central tenet of writing on the Web — and a sharp con-trast to traditional journalism, which breeds in writers and columnists the idea that they know more than their readers. The Web breaks down such conceit.

rgneva Does this leave us with a fractious babble in which many *rumeur* voices shout to be heard? No. Some voices will always

rise above others, depending on what they say and how
well and convincingly they say it. All sorts of cultures
produce leaders.

seulement

The goal isn't merely an aggregation of many unfiltered
opinions. Instead of the on-the-one-hand, on-the-other
tradition of Objectivity, to which the traditional press pays
obeisance, we seek a new **informed subjectivity,** one in
which point of view is prized, not hidden.

Informed subjectivity preaches opinion that is fair, openly
acknowledged, and clearly argued—that is drawn from
facts and research.

Rassembler

This kind of subjectivity is more, not less, professional: It
encourages journalists to do more than pass along unresolvable arguments. It asks them to gather facts, organize
them, and present them in a persuasive and useful way,
so readers understand the journalist's conclusions and how
they were reached.

les foutaises
"cachées"

CYPHERPUNKING... AND DEBUNKING *le démenti*

When other journalists ask me about writing on the Web,
their first questions invariably center on the anger and
confrontation so prevalent there. Is hostility endemic?

Anger and confrontation **are** cyberspace staples. Founded *produit*
mostly by male geeks, hackers, and oddball researchers, *excentriq*
Net discourse can get confrontational, assaultive, and
patronizing. Untempered testosterone rules. The Net has
no history of organized communication, none of the
parliamentary traditions that have served the British for
centuries, none of the patrician politesse that guided the
Founding Fathers' passionate debates over the Constitution.

If the Net has any legacy at all, it is one of anarchy, of chaos,
of the belief that all information should be free. While this
is a powerful, even stirring, political idea, it doesn't do *émouvant*
much to construct a civic framework on which to build a
coherent community.

The Net also has a legacy of anonymity. Cypherpunks—radical
proprivacy geeks who support techno-anarchism and the

right to anonymity—epitomize this ideal. Cypherpunks are a phenomenon unique to this medium and may have paved the way for the mindless verbal violence found here. Their original purpose—to promote unfettered access to information—defied the very notion of civil discourse. In fact, their treasured anonymity defies even the notion of discourse: If cypherpunks wanted real discussion, they'd reveal their identities and invite response, as most flamers do. They are among media's rarest and at the same time most easily recognized subspecies: nihilists.

Anonymous communication encourages verbal violence. It's far easier to attack someone and question personal motives when the social consequences of face-to-face verbal assaults are removed.

Add to this the speed of Net communication: Seduced by the instantaneous ability to Send, people pop off when their tempers flare. They often don't take the time to cool off, reflect, or take a sound look at the messages they mail and post. Hostile messages are often impulsive and frequently regretted.

Since the Net makes communication so easy, it makes debate inevitable. Nobody who writes or posts on the Web should expect anything less than repeated challenge. In fact, the notion of critique, however heated, is **integral** to the work of Web writers and posters.

But I've noticed a strange phenomenon: When I respond quickly and respectfully to assaultive messages (those packed more with vitriol than critique), most hostile emailers either apologize, change their tone, or write back in a more reflective, serious, or friendly mode. Most of these posters are stunned that anyone read their mail or, even more amazingly, responded to it.

"I didn't think anybody would read this," states the typical comeback to my reply. Or, "I didn't think anybody would actually respond." These critics usually continue to disagree, sometimes vehemently, but their tone changes. When there's a **person** at the receiving end, posting becomes less confrontational and insulting. Many of the worst flamers would never assault anybody in another context. In fact, they can become supportive correspondents, and, in some instances, friends.

This rapid evaporation of surface hostility suggests that much of the alienation we read about among the young or among voters is myth. It is a disconnectedness from institutions—the experience pretty much everyone has with mass media—that breeds anger and frustration. The most vicious and personal flames reveal how detached media institutions have become. People have no expectations of being heard or answered, since they don't see their targets as individuals but as faceless parts of some larger and hostile institution—whether that be Wired Ventures, Microsoft, The New York Times, or just "the media."

Reader reaction is carefully contained in mainstream journalism; flaming is almost unheard of—and rarely given column inches. **So the animus behind posts on the Web serves as a healthy antidote to media arrogance and elitism.**

Writing on the Web—and about it—suggests new possibilities in the way we communicate with one another. For one thing, writing on the Web teaches—clearly and repeatedly—that few issues are simple and one-sided. So much information and criticism pours in after columns are written—more than was ever conceivable before the Net—that rigid positions seem, well, just rigid. Writers needn't be "correct." Positions evolve. Points are learned. Columns become living entities rather than fixed, indeed passive, declarations.

Since when have you seen politicians, advocates, or lobbyists change their minds or admit they were wrong after learning new information? Almost all divisive social issues—abortion, crime and justice, gun control, welfare, taxation, race—become eternal debates between special interests, lobbyists, and spokespeople. **Crossfire** becomes the model. The participants depend on their immutable positions for a seat at the table. As a result, most public discussions filtered through the media come through as balanced but contentious and unresolvable.

That cypherpunks and flamers deflate egos, challenge corporate authority, and diminish the power of pundits is healthy—it's precisely what's missing in traditional media. That they argue with personal attacks is unacceptable, because this prevents the evolution of rational, safe, and respectful discussion in the emerging culture of digital communications.

GIVE ME COMMUNITY OR GIVE ME DEATH

In online communities like The Well, where arguments rage for years and free speech thrives, coherent discussions are much more possible than on Web sites like The Netizen. On The Well, designated "hosts" monitor discussions, keep participants on topic, encourage disagreement (discouraging hostility when it crosses certain boundaries), and some-times even remove ("scribble") the worst personal attacks.

Even though some participants use pseudonyms, they cannot hide behind anonymity. Over time, many Well members come to know one another and begin to see themselves as part of a community.

Monitoring discussions is an inevitable step for any Web site that takes itself seriously or wants to be taken seriously. Somebody must provide oversight, be responsible, take charge. When that happens, flamers tend to retreat to the many thousands of places on the Net where flaming is the primary currency of communication. They are not being deprived of freedom—they are actually encouraged to go where they can find more.

Hostile posts invariably come from young, white, educated, and technologically literate (thus probably affluent) men. Although women will disagree vehemently and are clearly online in greater numbers today, they tend to focus much more on issues than on personalities in public discussions, and, in my experience, in email.

Women post in Threads far less frequently than men, yet roughly 60 percent of my email is from women. (Women and men have been buying computers in roughly equal proportions.) Many women have let me know that they find the confrontational, assaultive, patronizing style of Threads to be demeaning. Others find that the dismissive ethic endemic in public areas of the Net chills free speech, making it less free for women, the elderly, and the shy.

A primary test of the Web's maturation will be whether or not its public forums reflect broader chunks of the population than the men, most of them white, who patched together the Internet and developed its early communications ethos.

Of course, as the Net becomes corporatized, the Web will become more middle class. Companies like Microsoft will produce sites like **Slate**—rational environments that sustain communities of affluent subscribers who can pay to get in and whom advertisers want to reach. The Web will civilize itself.

This is pretty much how newspapers and the evening news got so dull. But Web aggression isn't likely to disappear entirely. The Net has too many distant and inaccessible outposts for civilization to conquer them all.

In fact, the most revolutionary aspect of Net media ecology is its grass roots. The first computer bulletin boards were founded by hackers, students, and other small cadres who patched together primitive media communities. **With a computer and a modem, everyone becomes his or her own publisher.**

Someone who is disenchanted with **The New York Times** probably can't get hold of a printing press. Someone who doesn't like NBC News can't go start a TV network. But anyone with the most elemental computer technology can create a computer bulletin board or conferencing system, throw together a Web page, or start a newsgroup.

The Net is composed of infinite individual slices.

TALK OF THE TOWN

In a September issue, **The New Yorker**'s brilliant and curmudgeonly cultural critic James Wolcott asks the central political question for old and new media: Is interactivity a good idea?

Interactivity is the bitterest pill for most mainstream journalists to swallow. Although it is often narrowly and mistakenly defined by writers like Wolcott as "audience participation," it is, in fact, a much bigger notion.

The New Yorker, for example, is the antithesis of interactivity, as Wolcott's essay reflects. It exists on a high cultural perch, sending observations, essays, and reviews down to the masses below. It publishes a few short letters to the editor, but otherwise readers have no input of any sort. Nor is there any simple way for readers to communicate with the magazine's editors and writers. Although nobody would say so, this clearly seems like a publication that doesn't relish the idea of hearing from too many of the foul-mouthed and unschooled masses. Its objective is to talk, not listen.

This is a model unlikely to survive long in the next millennium.

Interactivity in media means the redistribution of power. It means journalists, columnists, editors, producers, and pundits have less power to set editorial agendas and voice opinions than they used to, and individual consumers of media (you) have more. It means journalists have to really listen to their readers, not just pretend to.

Although many media—TV talk shows, radio call-in broadcasts, op-ed pages with email addresses—appear to be interactive, few really are. Faxes, call-ins, 800-number polls, and audience participation broadcasts involve audiences and the public to a greater extent, but they aren't really interactive: Producers and editors still tightly control access and content.

"Interactivity flings the airwaves open to the great, throbbing passions of the citizen-viewer," writes Wolcott, "and promotes active involvement rather than passive consumption—that is, it should remove some of the glaze from America's eyeballs. Nice idea, but in practice, it almost never works. I've seldom seen a talk show where

taking phone calls provided extra bounce or illumination."
Wolcott cites a number of dumb calls to **Larry King Live** and
C-SPAN as proof of why interactivity is failing.

This is disingenuous. **Larry King** is interactive only in the
sense that he talks to callers at all. But his broadcast—the
desk, his style, his control of the content—is anything but
interactive. His producers pick the guests and screen the
callers. He gets to cut callers off whenever he wants and
asks many more questions than they do. When he's sitting with a guest, he dominates both the format and the
discussion.

To use King's broadcast as an example is to misunderstand
interactivity's application and meaning.

Substantive interactivity is practiced only online. On Web
sites like Abbe Don's in the Cyborganic Gardens, where
people can read oral histories; on SeniorNet, where the once
voiceless elderly can form a community; on **Salon, Suck,**
and HotWired, where columnists exist only in conjunction
with their readers, not in place of them; and where public
forums varying wildly in quality and coherence are provided
side by side with columns and content.

On balance, interactivity is the most interesting idea to
come out of media in many years. **Interactivity is a stirring,
reinvigorating opportunity for journalism, which is, by every
account, disconnected from and increasingly disliked by people
who consume it.** Interactivity forces writers to confront
mistakes and poorly conceived notions or even change
their minds. It gives readers a real, rather than illusory,
sense of participation and proprietorship—one reason
many Net dwellers love their media and so few consumers
of old news do.

Although the American press was founded as an intensely
interactive endeavor by pamphleteers, poster makers, and
letter writers, modern journalists have become comfortable
with the idea that their audience is intrinsically dumber
than they are. No wonder the media are alienated from the
American public. Interactivity isn't a new gimmick for the
new media—it's a possible salvation for the old.

MAN BITES DOGMA

The lines between passionate belief, ingrained faith, and absolutist dogma are pretty thin—with the latter almost always growing out of the first two.

After all, dogma—the authoritarian, arrogant assertion of principles—demands that adherents not think about issues or articles of faith but accept them totally and eternally. And dogma can be found at the heart of the politically correct left and the rabid right.

Dogma is also encroaching on the Web, which considers itself the epicenter of free speech in America. And the threat of dogma is just as menacing in cyberspace as in the "real" world. Many on the Web hold, for example, that freedom of information should be absolute and without boundaries, that any curbs on any speech for any reason are unthinkable.

It is considered an unfortunate by-product of freedom, not an unacceptable curb on free speech, that many people are afraid to speak publicly online.

"It's too bad that people are afraid to post messages," a Netizen writer emailed me last week. "But that's the price we pay for freedom, isn't it? That isn't going to change." The writer's statement was understandable—a defense and celebration of the Web's most sacred principles. But it was dogma, too: the reflection of an absolutist belief that can't ever be challenged or debated.

If the digital world has a sacred cow, it's the notion that all information and opinion must be free, all the time. But what is **freedom**?

Truly free communities have a responsibility to go sacred cow tipping occasionally. While we're still basking in the glow of the Net's CDA triumph, this seems as good a time as any to ask, Do we need censorship here in cyberspace?

Political sites like this one are evolving dramatically into new kinds of political spaces—common gathering grounds where visitors are treated as citizens and members of a political community and thus need a place to meet and communicate safely in public. Confident and veteran Net dwellers often post intelligent, sometimes brilliant, posts and comments in public forums. But these discussions also attract obsessive debaters and sometimes obviously disturbed people hiding behind pseudonymous handles. Discussions are easily diverted, abandoned, or interrupted. Thoughtful, articulate people capable of adding immeasurably to the global civic debate such forums ostensibly foster are sometimes forced to turn away in disgust in the face of personal attacks and ill-considered, pointless rants.

For many people, the only thing to do safely here is read the opinions of others. For an interactive medium, this isn't nearly good enough. This isn't freedom.

While the libertarian streak on the Net is its most appealing and stirring ethic, one of its sad legacies is that **many of the Net's "civic" spaces are nasty, sometimes pointlessly and insufferably, hostile places.** Flaming, personal attacks, and eternal quarrels are now ingrained traditions—noxious habits that are not only tolerated but celebrated.

Media outlets such as HotWired routinely edit staffers and contributors like myself but refuse to edit public comments in their public forums. As a result, coherent, civil, and freewheeling discussions in these places is often impossible. What an ironic sacrifice to absolutist notions of free speech that many people do not feel free to speak.

This creates an impossible, sometimes hypocritical contradiction. We want you to post—we beg you to post—but we take no responsibility for anything that happens to you when you do. Please come and join our discussion, but if you get mugged and assaulted by craven fools unwilling to identify themselves, too bad. We're just helpless freedom fighters.

Let's be clear here: The Net has to remain free. There must always be plenty of places where people can express themselves—anonymously or otherwise—in whatever language or tone they wish.

But there must also be places where people are free to come together and speak civilly and rationally. Where they feel safe doing so. Where issues and concerns affecting the digital world—or any world—can be thrashed out over time, in a respectful, humane way. No political community in the history of the world has ever grown and prospered without a coherent and protected process that its members use to meet and talk with one another.

The miraculous power of this culture lies in the new ways it gives us to communicate with others. Much of the private email sent to me is stunning—rich, provocative, complex, thoughtful. If the most interesting comments were posted publicly, we would all share one of the smartest, most useful political forums in the world.

The miraculously overlooked weakness of this culture is that it doesn't offer a way to communicate safely. Too many people are put off by the sometimes barbaric environment of open forums.

They are, in effect, censored—not by moral guardians or congressional blockheads but by bullies and the civility-challenged. The ferocious libertarians of the Net rush to arms when told they can't use dirty words, but they snooze through this insidious, pervasive silencing of free speech and unbounded ideas.

Unfettered communication can thwart freedom rather than enhance it. Everyone has a right to free expression here—not just the people who constantly abuse it.

Like most self-described revolutionaries, the founders and rulers of the Net and Web tend toward arrogance and self-righteousness. They're quick to point out the many short-comings of the system outside and much slower to confront and acknowledge the failings and threats from within.

This is an enormous problem and a much more serious one than most people on the Web like to acknowledge.

The instinct on the Net is to deflate and challenge, not affirm and celebrate. Public forums on the Web don't exist to praise Caesar but to harass him. The more visible the writer or site, the more intense and unrelenting the criticism. The Netizen, for example, has gathered opinionated columnists and writers—Brock Meeks, John Heilemann, me—who are shooting their mouths off daily, and it lives on a widely visited site.

While it's much nicer to receive praise, **the critical, wary ethos of the Web is healthy; it mitigates against the sort of windy elitism synonymous with our most powerful offline media.**

Still, as The Netizen draws more attention from the mainstream media, it also draws more skeptics and flamers. Assaults by anonymous posters have paralyzed some of the site's public discussion. They have driven away many posters, derailed most reasonable discussions, and disgusted visitors.

"I would never post on your or any other public site," emailed a schoolteacher from Madison, Wisconsin. "I've been attacked so often and so viciously, often anonymously, I can't imagine why anybody with anything serious to say would [post]."

A columnist for a digital newsletter added: "I've given up posting anywhere in public on the Web. I guess if you're a 17-year-old boy, [the attacks are] cool. But I'm a professional, and I just find it intimidating." Those with livelihoods and reputations to protect evidently take less pleasure in name-calling combat.

Or this from an elderly man who has retreated to SeniorNet. "I can't keep up, really. Whenever you post something controversial or opinionated, you just experience this kind of cruel attack. They frighten me."

But the most frightening response came from a columnist on another Web site. "Trust me. Stop writing about this," he said. "You will just be the recipient of all sorts of vicious attacks. They'll run you off your own site. You're not really free to write about this, believe me."

It was a startling message from a veteran writer in a medium whose core belief is supposed to be that information wants to be free.

Time's Philip Elmer-DeWitt has been driven off many public sites on the Web and the Net because of his involvement in the magazine's infamous "Cyberporn" cover story. He is repeatedly and viciously attacked because people were outraged by his article and felt he didn't retract it quickly or enthusiastically enough. That the story was distorted and wrong is beyond question. That Elmer-DeWitt—one of the first journalists in America to take cyberspace seriously and explain it to the world beyond—has been silenced is a travesty.

In any other context, to be persecuted for something you write, driven off public discussion forums for your beliefs, or made to fear speaking out would be viewed as a direct assault on freedom of speech. Has freedom of speech come to mean posting only the opinions of young, angry males? Has it come to mean online discourse will be as one-dimensional as the worst political correctness?

HotWired will never drive flamers away. For all their obnoxiousness, flamers—like hackers—are an intrinsic part of Net culture. They often post intelligent and provocative opinions. They are badly needed deflators, tormenting the pompous and the powerful.

Is the answer to censor Threads? No.

The answer is to keep the free and open areas of sites such as The Netizen free and open. But perhaps creating a new kind of middle ground is also the answer—places where people seeking a civic community can do so in a more inviting environment.

In such places, posters would be required to provide at least their email addresses. Personal attackers and abusers would be discouraged and even prohibited if they became persistent. The community would recognize personal assaults as the threat to free speech that they are, members would aggressively police people who created a chilly environment for others, and they would vote to throw repeat offenders off the site. The community would take responsibility for and try to protect people who posted in good faith.

In time, Web readers will grasp the notion that the mainstream media model of opinion and debate—partisan, black-and-white, top-down, few-to-many, combative, confrontational—can be radically broadened. Perhaps the Web will become known as a place for dialogue, not diatribe.

GEEK REBELLION

CALLING ALL COMMANDOS

We were hoping to keep this under wraps, to operate in secret, but our hand was forced when Janet Reno and the Justice Department announced the creation of a cyber-force in June 1996 to combat terrorism on the Net. "Feds Ready Anti-Terror Cyberteam" proclaimed the headline in **USA Today.**

This left us no choice but to disclose the creation of Media Rant's Anti-Bullshit Delta Bravo Cyberteam (MRABDBC) to combat distorted reporting about the Net in the media, transparent posturing by politicians and police, pompous moralizing by windbags about dirty digital words, and the stampede by phobic boomers to protect their precious offspring behind a wall of V-chips and blocking software.

Rant's cyberteam is taking volunteers only. Only the bravest, toughest, and most resourceful netizens need apply. The rewards are few — maybe some cadged hardware and neat T-shirts. The risks are numerous.

Great sacrifice will be required. Force members will have to read and monitor waves of nuclear bullshit from the mainstream media about online perverts, hackers, thieves, pornographers, and, now, terrorists. Unit members will have to read countless stupid stories in papers and magazines about cyberporn, the dumbing down and isolation of children, and the demise of culture and civilization. They will have to watch hours of TV newscasts about lurking psychotics, bomb makers, and militia members waiting online to snatch and corrupt children.

Worst of all — be brave — they will have to read each and every one of William Bennett's best-selling fables about industrious bumblebees, brave eagles who soar over mountains, and hard-working frogs who can't wait to go to school.

Those who survive this will become a highly trained and

effective elite force. We will launch dangerous missions to harass and paralyze those who will distort information, profit off bigotry, or torment us. Our unit of veteran flamers will bombard moral guardians, journalists, and politicians with insulting print and electronic messagery until they retreat. Our cadre of granolaholic Whole Earth gurus will mail incomprehensible tracts and essays on the metaverse to editors and reporters. The Web's legions of obsessive digital debaters and quarrelsome dwellers will seize microphones at school board meetings, congressional hearings, and statehouse forums, causing even the born again to flee in terror. Sucksters will hurl venom at politicians and censors, haranguing congressional officers and whispering dirty words and provocative ideas into the ears of staffers.

Teams of hackers will undercut blocking software, liberate children, clear conferencing systems of censorship, and detract Janet Reno's cyberforce. Oh yeah, and **they'll create elaborate and impenetrable Net hiding places for warriors — and for refugees fleeing blockhead journalists, politicians, parents, and other windbags.**

We will amass our own arsenal — a daunting array of nerd and geek machinery: PowerMacs, ThinkPads, pocket penholders, calculators, modems. Who knows, we may even get working on the made-for-TV movie; we're thinking Johnny Depp and Rosie O'Donnell as the MRABDBC's fearless leaders.

We face many dangerous enemies with powerful weapons, lots of money, and big organizations. Out-to-lunch journalists and opportunistic politicians beware. Our MRABDBC force is out there. We are coming for you.

GEEK FORCE

The posts are pouring in.

"I hereby volunteer my services," messages Todd, the first volunteer for the Media Rant Anti-Bullshit Delta Bravo Cyberteam (MRABDBC).

"Send me mission orders and I'll sign up," emails Johan from
The Royal Institute of Technology in Sweden.

"I'll cover the Philippine side," volunteers Rubin from Manila.
"There are too many stupid politicos here who want to
censor the Net."

"I'm not much for flaming, but I'm at least as pissed off as you
are about the attempt to censor this glorious new medium,"
messages one reader. "Anarchy lives!"

While a New Jersey commando convert suggests a new,
crisper name for the unit: GEEK (Global Effort to Eradicate
Know-nothings) Force.

We like it.

Overnight, GEEK Force has operatives everywhere — a
secret force it would take a government decades to build.

In addition to the hackers, flamers, **Suck**sters, nerds, cyber-
gurus, and debaters that Media Rant suggests should
make up the unit, Web designers have emailed, protesting
that we are neglecting them and their ability to clog the
arteries of digital censors with state-of-the-art graphics and
video. Well, consider yourselves included. We have also
forgotten to include digital engineers and graphic artists,
who patch together the Web culture with tools we can't
even pronounce the names of, let alone comprehend.

We have asked the lords of **Wired** and HotWired to consider
GEEK Force hats, T-shirts, and other weaponry in the war
against the pious, the hypocritical, and the censorious.
They are mulling it over.

GEEK R.I.P.

Despite its promise, GEEK Force collapsed. It collapsed
mostly because The Netizen didn't have sufficient staff to
keep tabs on what amounted to its own international
media-watch group. A few Netizen staffers answered email
and struggled to keep the discussions going, but it was
impossible to pay as much attention to GEEK Force as this
miraculous gathering deserved.

Second, even though GEEK Force members signed up and posted frequently, it was not clear what the group's agenda should ultimately be or how it might be pursued.

And, most significantly, it was not possible to resolve these questions because The Netizen and HotWired have not faced the complicated question of how to create a rational environment for discussing the problems facing the digital community. GEEK Force was strangled by discussions that devolved into a kind of verbal dodgeball, where unrestricted flaming, personal attacks, and hostility were hurled without warning or, seemingly, reason. There are countless places on the Net for people to assault others, but how many public forums exist where those willing to honestly identify themselves can have rational conversations about common problems?

The Global Effort to Eradicate Know-nothings began as a joke. In my column I called for nerds, geeks, and other Webheads to respond to Janet Reno's creation of an anti-Net-terrorism commando force.

Lots of people took it seriously and volunteered, saying they were desperate to correct media distortions and untruths about the Web and the Net. It was an astonishing outpouring: It attracted political scientists, the elderly, college kids, Web designers, teachers from more than a dozen countries who wanted to join what they perceived to be one of the vigorous new political communities in the ascending digital nation.

Beneath all the great fun is a sober message — one that contradicts the common misperception that digital culture fosters apathy and civic disconnection. **If one measure of civic health is a willingness to fight for political ideals, the online nation is in far better shape than the exhausted offline political structure.**

Janet Reno et alia may prefer to cast the digital world as stupid, dangerous, and pornographic; they may cull images of a medium riddled with hackers, thieves, and terrorists; they may choose to ignore the likes of GEEK Force. And for a while, at least, they can.

The digital world is at a critical political juncture as we lurch toward the millennium. Corporations such as Microsoft are seeking to control the Web. Politicians are hoping to censor and regulate the Net. Fanatics are exaggerating the prevalence of sex online while distorting the diversity of the Net. Parents terrified by ill-informed journalists are scrambling to buy blocking software rather than teach their children how to use the Net responsibly. Major issues of access to the online world remain unresolved, while the gap between the technologically equipped and the technologically deprived continues to grow.

The self-destruction of GEEK Force suggests that an ethic created to ensure the free movement of ideas—and to hinder anonymous flaming and brutality—has become a form of digital fascism, one that inhibits free expression and makes civic maturation nearly impossible. If the communities of HotWired can't provide public meeting spaces for intense but respectful discussions of issues facing netizens everywhere, tepid corporate entities like Microsoft will seize the initiative. **If we leave it to *them* to tame the Net, we'll all end up with a top-down, pundit-driven, noninteractive, dull medium.**

GEEK Force embodied the richest fantasies of Net creators: a global coming-together of postpolitical citizens to do good. That sort of gathering is nearly impossible in media overwhelmed by corporatization and media monopolies, none of which give individual voices much of an opportunity to be heard.

Old media and old politics coproduce the national political system in America. They are incapable of invigorating the political process they've shaped so dramatically, one that has for generations excluded most individual citizens. The Net is a timely and desperately needed antidote to that alienation.

If there was ever a time when we needed more, not fewer, voices and more, not less, of that idiosyncratic pamphleteering, it's now. We're heading for 2000 and that famous bridge.

TECHNOLOGY AND PUNDITRY

TURBO-CHARGED

Even the most enthusiastic advocates of new media worry about some of the potentially toxic side effects on democracy—problems that present themselves clearly and frequently in the coverage of contemporary politics.

We live in an age of hypermedia, when our civic life comes rushing by at a speed far too fast for either comprehension or resolution. Politicians are up, then they're down; issues are critical, then they're gone; "Super" Tuesday becomes "Microscopic" Tuesday—all in a matter of weeks or days. We've lost track of our own political life. News, issues, polls, spin, and social upheaval travel through the culture at blinding speed, thanks mostly to new digital media and the reporters who have become overwhelmed, sometimes subsumed, by them.

Coverage of the 1996 campaign showed us that people are poorly served by journalists who bombard them with ceaseless, racetrack-announcer-style reports of political competitions, revolutions, and movements du jour. Reporters and pundits seemed neither to notice nor care that the significant development of one morning was totally at odds with what we had heard the week before.

Of course the people are restless! We're driving them crazy! This is a big problem for media new and old, and they all have to take some responsibility for it.

Thankfully, new media have reconnected many voters to the democratic process through computers, faxes, TV, phones, and radio. The new media have reinvigorated the practice of democratic discussion while breaking through the monopoly that journalists and pols held over political discussion. But the new media are also contributing to an overheated political atmosphere in which it is no longer possible to know the candidates and their values or to grasp new ideas and crucial issues before even newer ones come to the fore at warp speed.

R. W. Apple Jr. of **The New York Times** calls this the "turbo-charged" world of contemporary politics. Democracy was always meant to be deliberative, patient, careful, inclusive. Coverage of it was meant to be thoughtful, argumentative, and persuasive. Ideas took months, even years, to circulate and be resolved. Like teenage boys with big, new cars, the mainstream political media now seem addicted to sports, competition, noise, and speed — not comprehension, their most basic responsibility. Our politics are frenetic, overhyped. This isn't democracy at work, but democracy on speed.

STYLE OVER SUBSTANCE

Victor Frankenstein was a brilliant inventor, but he didn't think much about the meaning of his creation — until it was too late. As technology brings something, it always takes something away. Its particular wickedness is in so transfixing us with the miracle of discovery, we forget to consider the consequences.

In the midst of a presidential campaign, the conflict between invention and consequence is literally in front of our noses. We get information, news, the opportunity to build new communities, the tools to reunite with our political lives. We lose contact with politicians and we lack the time to think about issues — and the relative value of substance over imagery declines.

Presidential campaigns, more than any other national political exercise, remind us how technology — especially the omnipresent screen — has elevated image to a place of heretofore unimaginable dominance in politics. Image now dwarfs almost all other considerations in the selection of our most powerful leaders.

The videotape may be the most unintentionally political technology ever invented. It has changed almost completely the way presidential campaigns are conducted and how we receive our news of them. Before the rapid transmission of imagery, we had little choice but to focus on issues. Ever since, we've had little choice but to concentrate on imagery.

Bald, overweight, inarticulate, and ungainly candidates have largely vanished, no matter how honorable or smart they might be. Candidates must look presidential, whether they are or not.

Astute manipulators of media like Ronald Reagan can project warmth when there's no substance. Demagogues like Pat Buchanan learn to smile through their hateful messages and to spout ready-made, irresistible quotes. Candidates like Bob Dole learn quickly to abandon their own styles and voices and speak in the short, pithy, emotional "bite."

It's fashionable to blame the media for this distortion and superficiality. But the responsibility also lies with technology, which puts enormous pressure on the political process to generate vivid and compelling pictures but which fails to generate discussion or force a focus on issues.

In the digital nation, the issues posed by technology are front and center. Founded as a textual medium, the Net used to be made up of individually typewritten messages, ideas, and opinions. The digital nation has—at its core—been issue-driven, sometimes obsessively so. Urgent **communication** is at its heart.

But new technology is making the Web—and even the Net at large—less an environment of words and text and more a visual smörgåsbord. The Web is becoming more visual by the minute—from hypnotically beautiful Web sites, to newer graphical user interfaces, to better and clearer video transmission.

As graphics capabilities continue to evolve online, netizens need hindsight. Who wants another world in which everyone is pretty and, well, petty?

NOW *THIS* IS NEWS

After two endless political conventions, welfare is still dead, Hillary Clinton remains both loved and despised, Bob Dole is still boring. And journalists are stuck in the Big Muddy: They really can't do much more than emcee somebody else's show and try to justify their presence by investing it with drama and import that it obviously doesn't have.

If political conventions give you a view of only the lifeless twitching of Dead Media, go to the Weather Site on AOL to see a bright, breathing example of how Live Media are transforming the news.

The approach of Hurricane Edouard had some relevance to people. It could have destroyed property, disrupted work, even taken lives. On the Weather Site, the story unfolded in an intensely interactive, informative, and living way—with a hive of news and weather discussions that included forty-eight topics and more than ten thousand messages.

The Weather Site offers news in the most basic sense: almost-instant updates, information from hundreds of sources, and discussion. Meteorologists, scientists, storm-trackers, Air Force officers, and hundreds of private citizens gathered around the Weather Service Corps' Hurricane Center site to trade information about Edouard and to chat live about where the storm would hit, how previous storms have behaved, and whether trips, flights, or cruises should have been canceled or altered. The experts brought precise theories and fresh facts to the ever-wondrous mixed bag of opinionated online addicts and weirdos. Chaos and clarity—the informational twins of the online world—existed side by side.

This was news at its purest and most historic—it brought people the freshest information about something that dramatically affected them, without the need for blow-dried anchors, talking-head bureaucrats, or pompous pundits. It shows how we can reinvent journalism via new technologies in a manner that is both useful and participatory. It upstages political coverage, revealing how remote, fake, and co-opted that coverage is.

Hurricanes and political conventions aren't the same thing, but both are news. One is a living story covered in a brand-new way, the other is merely moribund.

FOUR WAYS TECHNOLOGY HARMS DEMOCRACY

1. Screen and digital media move information too quickly. Issues, ideas, and proposals are instantly outdated and overtaken. Major issues—the flat tax, illegal immigration, economic insecurity—overwhelm us, then vanish. Breaking news is presented continuously and transmitted faster than ever before. The shelf life of a "major" story is about two days. (Remember Jessica Dubroff? Henry Foster?) The shelf life of an American political issue seems to be about one week, from Sunday talk show to Sunday talk show.

2. Media technology inevitably emphasizes visual imagery—pictures, graphics, color, clarity. In contrast to the ugly, still mostly black-and-white, front pages of newspapers, this is great. But graphics sometimes become ends in themselves rather than enhancements or explanations of ideas.

   In politics, this is especially destructive. Unconventional and unconventional-looking candidates have virtually vanished from presidential politics. Well-manicured images on TV—and, more and more, on the Web—can be pretty but pointless. Style replaces substance.

3. The wider scope of new media—TV, radio, some online discussion—fosters controversy and confrontation. Added to the mix is the **Crossfire** syndrome, which reduces all issues to "left" or "right" or buries us in stalemated (and well-compensated) spin doctors. Sound bites, the primary political currency of new and visual media, are now the accepted norm of political discourse, even though they are the literal antithesis of it.

   In the online world—which once prided itself on the open flow of ideas—rampant flaming and hostility chill political discussion.

4. Technology fosters elitism. As yet, comparatively few Americans have the time, money, machinery, and confidence to master the Internet. This creates even more media and information elites with superior access to information and research tools and thus to knowledge and political power.

   A corollary is that technology increases the corporatization of news: It has brought efficiency and access to media and has made journalism profitable.

**Visionless companies like Westinghouse, GE, Microsoft —
run mostly by greedy and arrogant men — see news as
compatible with their other products: lightbulbs, nuclear
submarines, and software.**

This sucks, profoundly.

FOUR WAYS TECHNOLOGY HELPS DEMOCRACY

1. New technologies are breaking the monopoly that journalism and the two major political parties have held
over the national political process and are giving people
greater access. Online and off, on talk shows and over
800-number phone lines, individuals can once again put
questions directly to candidates and debate the issues
with one another.

   The political forums of the better Web sites, online
services, and chat rooms are the most vigorous anywhere
in the public political spectrum. (Where else would you
be lucky enough to have SeniorNet and **Suck** in the same
medium?) These forums are far more substantive and
engaging than those offered by mainstream journalism.

2. Conventional windbags are always gassing on about how
the public doesn't care about civics anymore, but their
cynical view is refuted whenever political leaders appear
on one of the more interactive media forums. Instead of
having to respond to the narrow agendas of Washington
journalists, candidates spend longer periods of time communicating more directly with voters about the issues that
matter. It's all about exposure, stupid.

   Though **Larry King Live** may not be truly interactive,
media and academic snoots may deride such programs
that respect ordinary people and their concerns. On broadcasts like his, we get to make up our own minds about
what the candidates are really like rather than depend on
reporters to tell us.

3. Mainstream journalism is militantly moderate. Expression
is permitted only within the narrow confines of the "right,"
the "center," and the "left." In fact, people often have
more complex views: They transcend narrow stereotypes.
But cable TV provides new outlets. From the talk shows

on Black Entertainment Television to the satire on Comedy Central, from the often boring but thoughtful guests on C-SPAN to the sometimes rebellious and satirical programming on Nickelodeon and MTV News, we see not the loss of civic discourse, but its rebirth.

Then we have the online universe, the most diverse, opinionated, and obsessively issue-driven medium of all. The digital world is a teeming, global idea and communications mart, a round-the-clock World's Fair where new ideas are continually being displayed, transmitted, and debated.

4. If the nation-state seems pooped, and the conventional ideologies and parties appear to be out of ideas, technology offers us the chance to re-form into newer, smaller, and, we hope, more creative communities.

The young can talk to the young, gay teens to other gay teens, the elderly to the elderly, and, more and more, anyone to anyone. This offers the promise—if not yet the reality—of ending the fragmentation, polarization, and deadlock that seem increasingly to cripple our national political structure.

DEAD PUNDITS SOCIETY

THE IMPERIAL PRESS

One of America's great quadrennial media rituals is the decampment of the Imperial Press from Washington to explore the attitudes and feelings of "the people."

Like the great court of King Louis XIV of France, the encampments of the Imperial Press are spectacular, lavish, and formidable. The entourage includes producers, pundits, techies, camera operators, anchors, researchers, assistants, walking bylines, wannabes, groupies, and lesser national and local scribes.

Its members move in great herds to New Hampshire, Iowa, Arizona, New York, and other major primary states. They commandeer airplane flights, take over hotels and motels, clean out car rental agencies, charter giant trailers and vans, pack restaurants, and jam bars.

And they poke mikes in front of hapless people walking down the street. "What do I think of Pat Buchanan?" asked one woman in South Carolina, struggling to get bags out of her shopping cart and into her car while fending off a crew from CBS News. "Why, nothing. Is he the jerk or the good one?"

For the Imperial Press, the presidential election is serious stuff — not because of the politics, but because it is equal parts Super Bowl, World Series, the celebrity ball, and job fair. Its members get to yell at the candidates, sport passes on their shirts, be chauffeured around in buses and vans, get a good look at one another, and preen for the executives who fly in for a peek at the mayhem.

Like any court, the Imperial Press has its own pecking order: At the top are Dan, Tom, and Peter; then the gaseous pundits from the **Los Angeles Times, The New York Times, and The Washington Post;** then the screamers from the TV talk shows and the heavies from the newsmags; and at the bottom, the eager young writers anxious to see and be seen. Intense mingling is the order of the day, with everyone sharing and trading conventional wisdom and surveys like baseball cards.

The privileged few get to slip nonchalantly past the mounting security and Secret Service for time with the candidate and his handlers—for that extra, insidery spin that a pundit needs to stand out from the pack.

Every four years the Imperial Press reads the polls and surveys, then goes door to door to find people who reflect what the surveys say. Later comes some intense mood-gauging, which invariably reveals that "the people" are grumpy—worried about jobs, crime, taxes, and big govern-ment. (No political journalist ever got ahead by reporting that nothing much was happening.) The best part of this ritual are the reports sent "home" from real America. "Here in Arizona, Bryant, I'd say the mood is restless, unpredic-table," proffers one reporter on the **Today** show.

"What's the mood out there?" asks an earnest Bernard Shaw. "I'd say angry, Bernie," the CNN reporter in South Dakota dutifully responds. "Volatile. Worried about jobs and the economy."

(Why is it that every four years the Imperial Press is stunned that people don't like being thrown out of work, don't like being unable to afford health care, don't like seeing a slippage in real wages?)

I love the way the members of **the Imperial Press stand before the camera in all their color-coordinated, pompous, self-righteous, well-fed glory, while everyone they run into seems dyspeptic, constipated, and disheveled.** No doubt some of "the people" are also healthy, active, and reasonably content with their lives. We don't see them on TV too often, though—maybe they're busy working when the Imperial Press drops by.

PISSING IN OR JUST PISSING US OFF?

The Imperial Press has not always existed. American political journalism got its start in seventeenth-century England and

Colonial America — in writers such as John Locke, Francis Bacon, Benjamin Franklin, Thomas Paine, and Thomas Jefferson. They all advocated advancing social justice, especially individual rights of disenfranchised people.

Almost all early American journalists, pamphleteers, and publishers were first and foremost outsiders. To paraphrase LBJ's rural Texas eloquence, they lived happily outside the tent, pissing in.

Modern political journalism no longer believes in, or executes, the model of its progenitors. Much of the Washington-based political media have been tainted by their proximity to professional politicians, greed, incest, and elitism.

Presidential politics are now a **coproduction** of the press and the political parties. Each seems to have eyes only for the other. They have their exclusive conventions, secret understandings, arcane language. Journalists care nothing for issues or coherence, only the play-by-play and the fake interrogatories with which they pretend to be tough but which faithfully cloud any relevant or substantial political discussion.

The original, stirring notions of political journalism — raising hell, reporting the truth, advancing arguments in the public good — have been forgotten. Reporters no longer stand outside the tent: They live and work **inside** it.

Political journalists are a powerful and affluent social elite, occasionally interviewing "the people," but never including them. They have, collectively, precious little integrity. They promote divisiveness and confrontation above all things. Some of their best known practitioners take fat speaking fees from industries they cover, refuse to disclose their outside incomes, socialize with the politicians they are supposed to monitor, and take money from sleazy TV talk shows.

Objectivity has made it impossible for pundits to engage in impassioned arguments — they can only repeat the opinions of others. They cannot discuss anything that matters — crime, race, violence, technology, the role of the federal government — in any useful way.

This ugly, wasteful, and dissonant "political" exercise makes a potent argument for disconnection from it. What was there, in the 1996 campaign, for us to bring into our own lives and make any sense of?

Ironically, it is the digital culture, not the political culture, that the press relentlessly pillories as apathetic, civically disconnected, and isolated. How happy I was to get online last night. It felt like crossing the border from some strange and ugly Wonderland back into a raucous but safe and familiar place. It was occupied by people who would have torn to bits anybody who dared to present these campaign results with a straight face.

"WHAT WE MEANT TO SAY..."

An ingrained new-media phobia lies at the heart of journalism's anxieties about the digital world. Journalism is our Chicken Little, shrieking from papers, TV screens, and magazines that doom is upon us.

Last week, the Scripps Howard News Service ran a widely reprinted feature that began: "As use of the Internet increases, so have reports of computers creating havoc between husbands and wives." The column, which offered one anecdote but no statistics to support this striking notion, did manage, of course, to quote a publicity-hungry college professor (what is it about academics and therapists?) who said that chat rooms and bulletin boards can lure "casual" Net users into addictive behavior.

Last Wednesday, **The Washington Post** reported in a front-page story, "Hooked On-Line, and Sinking," that faculty studying the freshman dropout rate at Alfred University in New York have found that "nearly half the students who quit last semester had been logging marathon, late-night time on the Internet." The **Post** also reported that MIT will deny addicted students access to the Net whenever they try to sign on.

In fact, said the paper, colleges nationwide are discovering a "troubling side effect: A growing number of students are letting computers overwhelm their lives."

Now, here's a pointer from Media Rant: Whenever you read a front-page story like this, turn to the jump on page A-10 (or wherever) and look for a qualifying paragraph, invariably buried deep in the story. You've read a version of it a thousand times in similar jeremiads:

"It is hardly a crisis on any campus — yet. Some college officials say it is merely a fad, and not nearly as harmful as other bad habits students often fall prey to on campuses — such as binge drinking of alcohol. But concern over the issue is spreading."

If it's hardly a crisis on a single college campus and may merely be a fad, one of countless obsessions that sweep college campuses, then why is one of America's most important newspapers running a story about it on the front page, where crises, not fads, should appear?

If we weren't such impeccable libertarians, we'd be hollering for legislation to require media to publish a what-we-really-meant-to-say paragraph on anything having to do with culture or society—this would explain why the Internet-as-addictive-scourge story and similar tales routinely arise.

Media Rant's truth-in-media paragraph would read this way: "We know this story is absurd, and if you think about it for five seconds, you'll think so, too. But we seem to have lost the ability as a medium to cover the reality of change and to provide a sense of perspective and proportion to the various dangers facing us and our children. We do this because we have become increasingly lazy and more and more reliant on polls, spokespeople, academics, and therapists whose livelihood often depends on their interests being perceived as urgent and timely. Reporting on these doomsday scenarios makes us feel relevant and useful: Life is dangerously unpredictable, but we'll keep you safe if you read our perpetual warnings and promise not to forsake us for all this glitzy new online stuff. We continue in this manner even as the economics and demographics of our industry make it clearer with each passing day that we are becoming useless, irrelevant, and mistrusted precisely because of dumb reporting like this."

MICROPUNDITS

The corporatization of the news has been a tragedy for mainstream media and for American society. It undermines free speech far more than any government action or libel suit ever could.

The press as envisioned by its American founders — Paine, Franklin, Jefferson — was the antithesis of the modern corporation. It was individualistic, rebellious, idiosyncratic, and ferociously opinionated. It was expected to poke, pester, and prod powerful institutions.

That the media should increasingly be consumed by corporations is perhaps an inevitable consequence of capitalism. But the idea that companies like Westinghouse (CBS), General Electric (NBC), The Walt Disney Company (ABC), and now Microsoft could end up controlling the dissemination of news would have sent journalism's raffish founding pamphleteers leaping from the top of Independence Hall.

There was no fight over the destruction of the heart and soul of mainstream journalism. It was simply acquired by people like Al Neuharth, Larry Tisch, and Robert Wright — CEOs with marketing plans for souls.

Meanwhile, for all its chaotic flaws, the Internet has emerged as something of a miracle, a just-in-the-nick-of-time alternative, a return to the spirit of early American journalists. Individuals are free to speak up again, and they have plenty to say. They post, they publish homepages, they flock to fresh sites.

There has been an explosion of pent-up energy, debate, and creativity in the online world. Sometimes it is wonderful, sometimes it is obnoxious. But it is no accident that the Net and the Web have grown so quickly. Both present a thrilling, hypnotic option to the incestuous, obsessively marketed, dull offerings of the mainstream magazines, TV newscasts, and daily newspapers.

Never has there been a medium like the Internet, powered so much by individuals and embracing so fierce an ethos of equal access. The founders and users of the Net advanced the notion that they were constructing a new, democratic, many-to-many model of communication. Here the mega-companies might find a far more expensive, difficult, and hostile reception than they expected.

Into this media reality now plunges the ultimate American corporation. Microsoft is spending tens of millions of dollars to become a "global news provider" on the Web with its Web magazine, **Slate,** headed by former **New Republic** editor and **Crossfire** co-host, Michael Kinsley. **The Internet needs Microsoft and Kinsley about as much as it needs a nationwide power outage.**

Kinsley personifies the best and the worst of contemporary media. As a Washington columnist, he was insightful, fearless, often brilliant. As co-host of **Crossfire,** he helped pioneer and ratify the smarmy, opinion-for-hire Washington media culture that squeezed all debate of public issues into narrow definitions of "left" and "right."

More than anything else, Kinsley's defection to Microsoft to create **Slate** made the skeptical media elite sit up and pay serious attention to the Web. Kinsley is the spiritual leader of the edgy, smart, and narcissistic Ivy Leaguers who dominate many East Coast magazines and news organizations.

But Kinsley's new boss, Bill Gates, has the editorial vision of a tree stump. His editorial invasion threatens to bring his notoriously elemental value system — ruthlessness and greed — to the Web's editorial culture.

It will be interesting to watch the battle between the sanitizing megacorporations accustomed to ruling mainstream media and the Web culture of **Suck**sters, cypherpunks, cyber-gurus, cyborganics, and spiritualists. The outspoken and individualistic spirit of Web culture is closer to the early

American press, which was a raucous collection of idiosyncratic voices and candid viewpoints. Farmers, merchants, and political leaders wrote on walls, published pamphlets and handbills, printed newspapers and magazines.

Microsoft, Time-Warner-Turner, and other behemoths just may not grasp the difference between their visions of mainstream marketing and a free and robust press.

POWER LUNCH

One summer day, in a private dining room at the fabled Four Seasons on Park Avenue (a regular watering hole for the heaviest of media heavies), an extraordinary gathering took place. Wanna know how the Eastern media really work? How their values are coming soon to a Web site near you? Read on.

The purpose of the gathering was to introduce Nathan Myhrvold, then Microsoft's group vice president of applications and content and in-house champion of the company's mushrooming media involvement, to the wary zeitgeist monitors of New York.

The media establishment in the East has long been a closed club, made up of the right people who went to the right schools who have always run the most powerful media. It's no longer any different from banking, except that it's vastly more pretentious and hypocritical.

Media critics, for example, don't necessarily criticize media. They host it. **New Yorker** media critic Ken Auletta, friend and confidant of media moguls everywhere, cheerleader for Michael Kinsley's **Slate** (he wrote in **The New Yorker** that Kinsley was reinventing magazines on the Web), arranged this let's-get-acquainted lunch in which new media could meet old and Microsoft could chat up the lords of the Eastern media establishment.

Tina Brown was there. So was Howard Stringer, CEO of Tele-TV; Tom Brokaw of NBC; **New York** magazine editor Kurt Andersen; **Time** editor Walter Isaacson; Peter Kaplan of the **New York Observer;** Laura Landro

of **The Wall Street Journal;** Steve Shepard, editor of
Business Week.

According to several of the participants, Auletta set up the
lunch at the request of Microsoft publicists. "Ken hosted it,"
one participant confided. "He sees himself as pretty savvy
now, new-media-wise. He felt we should all meet Nathan.
And Nathan wanted to meet us and reassure everybody that
Microsoft was no threat to us. And he isn't, if you ask me."

How sweet of Ken.

Did this executive find it strange that a person who calls himself a media critic would take it upon himself to grease
Microsoft's transition into the media business or that this
critic would bring one of its top executives together with
New York media executives? Did he find it odd that editors
and producers would attend but not share the nature of
the lunch with any of their readers or viewers?

"Why, no. What do you mean?" the participant said, puzzled.
"It was just Ken setting up a lunch. I have no problem with
that. Do you mean journalistically?" The last word was
uttered with great if clueless incredulity.

The irony was probably lost on the others, too. Publications
like **New York** magazine, **The New Yorker,** and the **Observer**
scarf for nonmedia gossip and tidbits like starving rats
in a garbage heap. But juicy lunches like that one are considered uninteresting. (No one published a single word
about it.) The truth is, there was little news made there,
but the symbolism was overpowering.

The man from Microsoft assured his listeners, among other
things, that the world wasn't coming to an end—that just as
TV didn't wipe out radio, the Web and the Net weren't
going to wipe out magazines and commercial broadcasting.
It was an awkward, long, uncomfortable lunch.

The Easterners were neither reassured nor awed by
Myhrvold, despite Auletta's best efforts to ingratiate himself to both new and old media moguls.

Myhrvold is clearly not one of the right people who went to
the right schools, not in the media sense. He's a geek—a

physicist by training and a confidant of Bill's. He is chubby and bearded, prone to wearing khakis, blue shirts, and running shoes. Typical of the nerds who built the digital world, Myhrvold probably thought these people, with Auletta's ministrations, would accept him and the radical new thinking he and his culture represent.

He was wrong. **Nerds don't run media empires in New York. Not now — not ever.** Just ask Manhattan's lords of Media, who **bristled** as they climbed back into their cars and cabs.

"He was frumpy, a nerd," said one. "He was patronizing. This is the new world? I can't believe he was sitting there telling us about media. We all run successful media. Everybody at the table knew a lot more than he does. He doesn't know shit about media."

Another was kinder: "Nathan was a nice guy. He wouldn't last in New York a week. If he came here, he'd be lunch."

DEAD PUNDITS SOCIETY

Dear new-media consumers: Hats off to you. The votes are in. The Punditocracy is dead. You killed it.

Political journalism, one of America's most elitist, ethically challenged, and dysfunctional institutions, is collapsing. This is especially true of its most visible and powerful heavy hitters, the Pundits.

Throughout 1996, the conventional wisdom of this herd of political reporters was plain wrong. This institution has never seemed more useless or out of touch.

The Republican Revolution is over. Pat Buchanan did not tear the party apart. The voters were not as angry and paranoid as we were told they were. The Republican moderates did not revolt. The Clintons were not done in by scandal. Bob Dole's "bounce" was a media invention. Ross Perot is not wreaking havoc with anything.

If there was a big political story in 1996, it was perhaps the growing conviction that our existing political structures and the institutions that cover them are tired, inadequate, and unresponsive.

We and the world we live in appear to have outgrown claustrophobic political labels like Republican and Democrat or liberal and conservative. The words now work like powerful hay fever medication, leaving us sleepy and distracted.

One of the enduring realities of the 1996 campaign season was the demise, hopefully for good, of the Washington media culture that told us what to think. Theodore White, James Reston, Eric Sevareid, John Chancellor, and Arthur Krock are dead. David Brinkley, Hugh Sidey, Roland Evans, and Robert Novak seem unsure of what to say anymore. David Broder is writing books on how the system is broken. George Will writes most enthusiastically about baseball. And Michael Kinsley has vanished into the great and hungry maw of the Web.

It's hard to mourn the passing of this institution. Journalist-scholars like Walter Lippmann and I. F. Stone haven't been around for decades. The Punditocracy has lost its bearings in recent years, sometimes becoming richer, better known, and more powerful than the politicians it's supposed to cover. It has sacrificed dignity to sound bites and hoary Washington talk shows.

In past campaigns, individual reporters and writers—Curtis Wilkie, Richard Ben Cramer, Maureen Dowd—emerged in different ways to define candidates, campaigns, and the times in which they occurred. That didn't happen in 1996. No mainstream journalist emerged with a particularly original or compelling view of the 1996 campaign. It may never happen again.

The reason is you. You are getting your news and information from many different sources. You don't watch network news every night, and you don't read **The New York Times** or any paper's op-ed page every morning. You get some of your news online, some from radio, some from CNN. You read newsmagazines or other magazines from time to time, talk to your friends, read books about subjects that interest you. You soak up information through the ether, pausing to rummage for more when something catches your attention.

Because of your access to many sources of information, you are no longer at the mercy of a few networks, newspapers, or newsmagazines. The Web is much too diverse and vast for any single personality to dominate the way single journalists once shaped political coverage.

This is a reality that mainstream media — especially the variety rooted in New York and Washington — stubbornly refuse to accept.

The Punditocracy ratified candidates and issues, set the national agenda, anointed and rejected politicians. As the Punditocracy and its enormous power over our political world ends, we all may feel the enormous void its demise has left. But no one is as panicked as the Pundits.

They have not gone gracefully. Instead, they accused you of being civically dumb, apathetic, and ignorant.

Nuts to them. If the process they cover is tired, they are even more spent. Their time is up. They lost fair and square, in the best spirit of democracy.

You voted with your channel switchers, modems, keyboards, and time. And, in a landslide, you drove the pundits from their perches.

A PARABLE OF TWO PUNDITS

In 1992, new media — and new uses of old media — radically transformed the presidential campaign and seemed to be altering politics for good. Jerry Brown invoked technology as the voters' means to take back the political process. Ross Perot used Larry King Live as a national political platform. Surging conservatives used talk radio to invigorate the right. Comedy Central covered the conventions better than the networks did. And online technology appeared poised to reconnect alienated and disenfranchised voters to the political process through unprecedented open debate and vigorous democratic discussions.

Early in 1996, writer John Heilemann and I set out on

parallel media journeys for The Netizen. The concept was to track how the Web transformed the political process in the first wired election. Heilemann was to cover politics, the candidates, the conventions, and the campaigns. I would write about the media covering them.

Heilemann is a natural political journalist — clear, sharp, plugged-in, and energetic. Because he was writing on the Web, he was freer than most of his colleagues to say what he thought and felt. Yet Heilemann followed most of the rules. He took the process seriously, and he diligently tried to explain it. He traveled with both campaigns to the point of exhaustion, went to the primaries and conventions, lunched with insiders, listened to speeches, interpreted symbols, provided instant analysis, and searched for meaning. His writing suggested initially that he was excited to be covering a presidential campaign.

Things didn't turn out quite as we'd expected. Nineteen ninety-six was not the year of the Web, at least not in terms of mainstream politics. The culture wasn't yet big enough to affect the political process. The candidates didn't need it or turn to it as they had used new media like cable and faxes in 1992.

In 1996, new media played almost no substantial role in the presidential campaign. Larry King talked to movie stars and football players. And talk radio? Does anyone but blindered dittoheads remember or listen to Rush Limbaugh anymore? The Web proved a magnet for special-interest pages and for the media organizations we were trying to escape. **We witnessed big political sites looming out of the ether like rudderless ocean liners, offering slick graphics, static information, and worthless propaganda.**

The process didn't help. The election was shallow and hollow from the beginning. No one but Washington reporters ever got excited about it. By spring, it seemed clear to me that the campaign was a metaphor for all that doesn't work in both journalism and politics. I couldn't bear the **New York Times** pundits, CNN's politico-sports talk, the whoring Washington talk shows, the network stand-ups.

Heilemann struggled to make sense of the campaign; I just abandoned the attempt.

Why attend to those tired institutions when what was happening on the monitor a foot from my nose seemed so much more interesting? I watched fearsome debates, fresh ideas, a brand-new culture rising out of the primordial digital muck, its politics teeming with energy. How could a medium like this one have a major impact on a leaden process like that one? By focusing so obsessively on them, we missed a much more dramatic political story—us.

I focused instead on the new body politic—as reflected in interactive media and the digital culture. I was flamed, challenged, complimented, and stretched almost daily. The Web became my formidable and stern teacher, whacking me on the wrist with a ruler when I spoke too hyperbolically, didn't do my homework, or wasn't listening intently enough. And it comforted me when I struggled or seemed discouraged or lost. It taught me that Canadians and Argentineans and Italians look upon America in amazement and often approach the world in a completely different way. I earnestly looked for new kinds of Web sites, ones that redefined politics, biography, and religion, and I found them, from the Jesus Home Page to Abbe Don's loving biography of her grandmother on Cyborganic Gardens.

I argued with techno-anarchists about anarchy, flamers about civility, white kids about rap, black kids about the police and O. J. Simpson, **Suck**sters about attitude, journalists about media, evangelicals about sin. I was scolded by scholars and academics for flawed logic or incomplete research. I was shut down by mailbombers outraged by my criticism of Wal-Mart's music censorship.

I saw the strange new way in which information and opinion travels down the digital highway—it's linked to Web sites and passed on to newsgroups, mailing lists, college computer conferencing systems. **I saw my writing transformed from journalistic punditry to a series of almost-living organisms that got buttressed, challenged, knocked, and kneaded by the incredible volume of feedback suddenly**

available. I lost the ingrained journalistic arrogance that taught me I was right and my readers didn't know what was good for them. On the Web, I learned that I am never completely right, that I was only a transmitter of ideas waiting to be improved by people who knew more than I did.

Ideas almost never remain static on the Web. They are launched like children into the world, where they are altered by the many different environments they pass through, almost never coming home in the same form in which they leave.

All the while, I had the sense of Heilemann racing alongside like his soulmate the Energizer Bunny, carrying the real political weight, making points that had to be made, responsibly slugging his way through the campaign coverage, guiding the increasingly exasperated people who actually wanted to follow the election.

By the end, he seemed dispirited, even betrayed.

What John learned—and wrote—was that the political system he was seeing isn't functioning. It doesn't address serious problems, and the problems it does address are not confronted in a rational way. It doesn't bring us the information we need or take us toward comprehension or solution. The political ideologies that shape our political culture seemed on the verge of collapse.

"Nineteen ninety-six was the year that Old Politics died," Heilemann eventually wrote in **Wired** magazine. "Outside this bizarre electoral system that's grown and mutated over the past forty years—this strange, pseudo-meta-ritual that, experienced from the inside, feels like being trapped in an echo chamber lined with mirrors—there are profound, paradigm-shifting changes afoot."

Unencumbered by objectivity, Heilemann got it right. There are paradigm-shifting changes afoot: The young people who form the heart of the digital world are creating a new political ideology. The machinery of the Internet could create an environment in which the Digital Nation can grow and become a political entity in its own right.

They are becoming the powerful elite Francis Bacon foresaw four hundred years ago.

By covering the campaign, Heilemann was almost beaten down by its lack of meaning and purpose. There is nothing more exhausting than being stuck on a big story that dies on you, that you come to see, day by day, as pointless.

By avoiding the campaign most of the time, I ended up in a different and unexpected place. I had wandered into the nexus between the past and the future, the transition from one political process to the next. Hannah Arendt wrote that two things are necessary for the making of revolutions: the sensation of being free and the ability of humanity to create "a new experience which reveals man's capacity for novelty."

The Net qualifies on both counts.

Heilemann stayed with the campaign and ended up feeling bleak; I left it and ended up feeling upbeat. Heilemann came to believe he was attending a wake; I felt I was witnessing a birth, the first stirrings of a powerful new political community.

POSTPUNDITRY

POSTPOLITICS

POSTPOP

POSTPO
POSTPO
POS

THE BIRTH OF A DIGITAL NATION

WHY WE NEED WAY-NEW POLITICS

Hannah Arendt, in **On Revolution,** writes that the most exciting appeals to thought and reason in intellectual history occur at those odd, in-between periods she calls **intervals.** At such moments, historians, actors, and spectators all focus intently on things that **are no longer** and on things that **are not yet.**

One such interval was between the Dark Ages and the Enlightenment. Another was between the time monarchies ruled the world and the American Revolution, which sparked the concept of individual rights.

We live in that kind of time now, especially those of us who live and work online. Caught between the past and the future, we are precariously balanced on the fault line between the ideas and institutions that are fading and those that have not yet fully revealed themselves.

The Industrial Age, rusty and tired, is on the skids. The Nuclear Age failed to materialize. The Space Age lasted barely twenty years before we discovered we didn't have compelling enough reasons to make the trip. Swept up in the deepening disenchantment between our current political system and the onrushing millennial hype, we can hear and feel the plates shifting.

Those of us in the digital culture pose great questions but have few answers. Are we a powerful new kind of community or just a mass of people hooked up to already obsolete machines? Are we living in the middle of a great revolution, as some have suggested, or are we just another passing arrogant elite talking to ourselves? Do we share common goals and ideals, or are we the next ripe jackpot for America's ravenous corporate media machine, already hungry to build the machines that drive our world and to write the programs with which we communicate?

Add to these the toughest question of all: Do we signify a new kind of politics? **Can we construct a new kind of civil society with our powerful new gadgets? Or are we just a great, wired babble collectively pissing into the digital wind?**

I believe we are at the beginning of a new age.

The old political system is not just decrepit. It is, in many ways, dead. Pundits from new and old media alike shared this view in the postmortems of the 1996 presidential campaign. Almost nobody who came near this exhausted process left thinking our system is working or can survive in its current state for long. The offline political culture was a desiccated world of C-SPAN talking heads, bland bureaucrats, and pompous pundits. The public was not just alienated from the manner in which media and political parties presented our political process but utterly disconnected from it.

Against this backdrop is the breathtaking energy, community, and commerce of what I call the Digital Nation.

On the Net over the past year, I have seen the love for liberty reborn. I have seen political discussion thriving, rights fiercely articulated and ardently defended. I have seen a culture crowded with intelligent, educated, politically passionate people who line up to express their civic opinions and participate in issues debates. I have seen netizens learn new ways of political communications. I have seen the beginnings of a New Rationalism, made possible by the kinds of communities and communications that, more than any piece of machinery, are the miracle of the Digital Age.

Forget politics as we have known it. The postpolitical ideology of the Digital Nation starts not with government but with community.

WHY WE CALL IT POSTPOLITICS

As the millennium approaches, the digital community— with its money, education, technological skills, energy, the world's greatest system of communications, and access to the world's information — will become an extraordinarily powerful factor in determining the civic life of the entire planet.

The postpolitical future holds some changes in store:

1. No longer will netizens expect existing governmental structures, institutions, parties, or legislative bodies to solve social problems and complex economic issues.

2. Sexual orientation, gender, and race will matter less than ever before. The new digital generation is the first generation to experience diversity and pluralism throughout their lives.

3. Companies will be viewed not as greedy villains but as can-do partners in building a new culture and political structure.

4. The citizens of the Digital Nation are, for the most part, affluent, educated, and self-absorbed. They often work and live apart from many of the country's worst social problems and underclass crises. They are mobile but tend to cluster in coastal enclaves. They have more disposable income and leisure time than almost any other social group. They are an elite.

5. The Digital Nation isn't Democratic or Republican, knee-jerk liberal or stridently conservative. It values personal responsibility and opportunity. Its citizens tend to attach themselves to ideas rather than parties. Its members reject both the PC rhetoric that has crippled liberalism — and much of journalism — and the heartless and fanatical moralizing that has warped conservatism and the Republican Revolution.

6. It is libertarian. No generation since that of Paine and Jefferson has committed itself more clearly and urgently to the notion that information should be free, and that there are no boundaries for what can be said about religion, politics, or social issues. This generation believes that the vendors and users of information have a more equal relationship to one another than ever before.

7. The digital generation is allergic to moralizing and preaching. It has been warned, lectured to, insulted, and patronized—from William Bennett's stultifying moralizing to preachers', journalists', parents', and teachers' obsessive clucking about the dangers of sex, TV, drugs, computers, alcohol, and music. As a result, this generation is almost impervious to sermons. People of this generation believe what they see, read, and hear—not what people tell them they should be seeing, reading, and hearing.

8. Attitude, informality, and humor are the Digital Nation's basic tenets. Popular culture is viewed not just as entertainment but as a common language and a shared point of reference. The digital generation doesn't have big ideas about poverty, the underclass, crime, education, or other social issues.

Of course, many do hope that the new community—which includes information-sharing, creativity, and the intensely democratic participation of individuals made possible by the rise of the Net and the Web—may be able to define political problems and find creative solutions. At the same time, the Web and the Net are intensely fragmented and diverse, and the entropy implicit in the medium may defy the forging of unifying ideas or common political goals.

BIRTH OF A NEW NATION

Two hundred years ago, the passage of a noxious Stamp Act, through which the British Parliament attempted to unfairly tax its colonists, became a catalyst, creating a political consciousness among Americans and sparking the American Revolution.

On February 1, 1996, the Digital Revolution was handed its catalyst. On that "Black Thursday," Congress passed (with Clinton's endorsement) a sweeping telecommunications reform bill including Internet censorship provisions that made a shambles of the First Amendment.

The sanctimonious champions of the Communications

Decency Act argued that the legislation would protect children from exposure to pornography. But their agenda was far broader and more insidious. The CDA attempted to criminalize the transmission, posting, and distribution of "indecent" material to the World Wide Web, FTP sites, Usenet newsgroups, or BBSes. Private email or online chat-room communications with anyone under eighteen were covered by identical provisions. As punishment, it would have meted out a $250,000 fine and up to two years in prison.

The CDA was as abhorrent to the online world as the Stamp Act was to eighteenth-century colonists.

It galvanized the Net community, turning it into a political force willing to fight for its own interests. Cursor potatoes took action. **Web sites were bordered in black, Congress members were mailbombed, and even mainstream newspapers put pictures of placards reading "Uncle Sam Out of My Home-page" on their pages.**

Fortunately, on June 12, 1996, the U.S. Court of Appeals for the Third Circuit declared the CDA unconstitutional.

"Unlike traditional media, the barriers to entry as a speaker on the Internet do not differ significantly from the barriers to entry as a listener," the judges wrote. "In the argot of the medium, the speaker can and does become the content provider, and vice-versa. The Internet is therefore a unique and wholly new medium of worldwide human communication."

Chief Judge Sloviter argued that the CDA clashed with "our most cherished protection—the right to choose the material to which we would have access." Judge Stewart Dalzell added: "The Internet has achieved, and continues to achieve, the most participatory marketplace of mass speech that this country—and indeed the world—has yet seen. The plaintiffs in these actions correctly describe the 'democratizing' effects of Internet communication: Individual citizens of limited means can speak to a world-wide audience on issues of concern to them."

Dalzell concluded that "the Internet deserves the broadest possible protection from government-imposed, content-based regulation" because, as he put it (paraphrasing a famous line of Justice Felix Frankfurter's), **"Any content-based regulation of the Internet, no matter how benign the purpose, could burn the global village to roast the pig."**

Thanks to the dunderheaded political posturing of our elected leaders, a fractious, fragmented, diverse collection of individuals, businesses, and communities was united for the first time. The CDA forced the digital culture to see itself as a separate entity and to defend the freedoms, privileges, and traditions it has patched together in recent years. It made clear that the values of the Net differ profoundly from those governing much of the country.

LIVE UNCENSORED OR DIE

The censors are losing their clout.

Though it may be easy to spook big corporations into dumping their controversial online content, it's becoming nearly impossible to monitor or close down individuals with even limited access to new digital cable or computer technology. Most 12-year-old citizens of the Digital Nation can outwit Clinton, Bennett, or the Senate's James Exon.

Information technology is guaranteeing censorship's obsolescence. Chase a show off CBS and it pops up on Comedy Central. Block a digital file with "sex" in the title and it will be renamed and encrypted in a different form. Drive rap out of Time Warner and it will reappear on one of a hundred willing labels. With the computer and the modem, technology has finally outrun the legions of the self-righteous who, throughout history, have been eager to step forward and tell us what we should or shouldn't think, read, see, or hear.

More than any other medium, the Internet is shattering any real control over communications. **If Iraq, China, and Iran cannot control email, how can the FBI?** The Net already skips across borders and transmits countless billions of individual messages a day. Computers, software, and

modems allow tiny groups of people to form their own
digital communities and conferencing systems—and to
re-create them again and again, if necessary.

The news that censorship—one of the oldest notions in information—is falling apart is a landmark political story if ever
there was one. It's a story that goes untold, however, in
the mainstream press. Journalists have tragically failed in
recent years to make the vital connection between free
speech for the press and free speech for rappers, children,
TV producers, and the digital world. Instead, they have
created a climate in which new media have been viewed as
dangerous or destructive—and in dire need of censorship
and control.

Why? Because the defeat of the censors is profoundly threatening to the broad coalition of institutions—educational,
political, religious, parental, journalistic—that have governed
us for centuries and controlled the movement of ideas.

WATERSHED MOMENTS

It was no accident that both the **Time** cover story on
pornography in cyberspace and Congress' Communications
Decency Act were debunked and disemboweled in the
space of one year.

When **Time** magazine ran its now famous "Cyberporn" cover
in July 1995, suggesting that cyberspace was overrun
with child-stalking perverts, it made journalistic history,
though not the kind it intended.

On The Well, cyberjournalists Mike Godwin, Brock Meeks,
and Donna Hoffman worked together—without organization
or coordination—to debunk the phobic story and shoddy
research that supposedly supported it. Elsewhere, on sites
like HotWired, reporters demonstrated how quickly accurate information could be gathered and shared on the
Web. Within hours, more (and more accurate) information
was available online than in the mainstream press. It
marked one of the first time people turned **to the Net** for
their news.

The balance of power between new and old media was forever altered.

Time never fully retracted its flawed report, but it did acknowledge that it should have taken a closer look at the methodology behind it. For one of journalism's most arrogant institutions, this was akin to a blubbering apology.

Years of such phobic and distorted reporting about new media culture and the Net have created a political climate in which some Americans actually believe that screen-driven media is responsible for some of our worst social problems, including violence. Is it such a surprise that, in this climate, Congress passed the blatantly unconstitutional Communications Decency Act to muffle the Internet?

Of course, the effort backfired on Congress, much as it backfired on **Time** editors. Perhaps Congress members have begun to gather that the digital culture is no longer a faceless band of geeks but a powerful community with access to information, organization, and, most importantly, one another.

But the online reaction to the CDA, and the subsequent political mission of netizens, did more than just defeat a bad bill. The CDA provided the Net and Web communities with an urgent need to **defend** a shared belief —that information wants to be free—and to begin to **define** the values of the online community.

The CDA never seriously threatened free speech, but it helped this new political force to coalesce and lift the digital world out of its self-absorption.

Just as the British tea tax inspired American colonists, the CDA gave the digital world an identity as a separate nation. It raised precisely the same question the colonial patriots asked: **How can any community be governed rationally by a remote and arrogant authority?** It revealed the presence of a collective system of moral values worth fighting for and a vital, ascending community willing to fight.

In the most profound way, the CDA struggle focused attention on the Internet as the locus of free speech and civic discourse: The federal courts, in the CDA ruling, described the Net as "a far more speech-enhancing medium than print" and as "the most participatory form of mass speech yet developed." This is a stunning declaration, a landmark in the evolution of the digital world as a political entity in its own right.

Utopians have always tried to foresee the specific ways in which technology will transform and save the world. That's why academics call them the "fools of history"—technology and the ways in which people use it are inherently unpredictable.

But the Net bristles with promise: It may very well become a central forum for informed and civil civic debate, a medium in which individuals are reconnected to one another and the democratic process they share. It is also a vehicle for transmitting rational thought and truth instead of the paralyzing dogmas that have so disfigured our political process.

THE BODY POSTPOLITIC

DIGITAL DEMOGRAPHICS

At its young and affluent heart, the online community is libertarian, educated, materialistic, worldly, tolerant, rational, technologically equipped, and blissfully disconnected from conventional political organizations. Narrow labels like liberal and conservative don't apply.

Economically conservative, this community is also committed to the notion of pervasive business opportunity. Despite being wary and sometimes cynical about public life, the members of this community—netizens—are more optimistic about their lives and futures than their elders are.

And while the Digital Nation is clear about what it doesn't like—for example, both government and media are seen as corrupt, irrational, and ineffective—it's not yet clear what overtly political values netizens share. Nevertheless, the viability of its postpolitical ideology grows—not only in the many opinions expressed online, but in demographic and social surveys assembled by think tanks, polling organizations, and research groups.

For example, **American Demographics** magazine published the results of one such survey in its September 1996 issue. Developed by the Brain Waves Group of New York City, and conducted by Market Facts of Arlington Heights, Illinois, the survey's results will ring true to regular Net users and watchers.

First off, the study found that while Americans are fragmented and divided on countless issues, the number who share common values is surprisingly large: Two-thirds say that having close relationships with other people is always on their minds. Half say the same about security and stability, and almost half are intent on having fun. These are the three most important shared values regardless of age, sex, race, income, or religion.

Americans, the survey found, are not as self-centered as presidential candidates obviously think they are. Only one-third are thinking much about having the power and influence to get what they want or about developing themselves as individuals.

Still, the study divided Americans into four distinct subcultures: self-navigators, post-yuppies, family-values boomers, and hard-core traditionalists.

- More than half of the self-navigators are younger than 35—many were born after 1970—and they add up to about 26 percent of adults.
- Post-yuppies represent 29 percent of adults: They're concerned with achievement and power; are intensely individualistic; and are recognized by their identification with such yuppie values as affluence, upward mobility, and conspicuous consumerism. They are no longer young, are as likely to be suburban as urban, and face the very real threat of being downsized out of their jobs.
- Family-values boomers make up just over a quarter of the population and most closely resemble those of that cliché, "the average American," according to the study. They enjoy their relationships, traditions, and lives, and they think little of—or about—power and achievement.
- The hard-core traditionalists represent 18 percent of adults and tend to be older and more conservative. They embrace tradition. They conform.

In 1996, both major political parties tailored their campaigns almost exclusively to the hard-core traditionalists (Dole) and family-values boomers (Clinton). This explains why there was so much blabbering about values and family in the presidential election campaign and why everybody else felt so disconnected from the process.

The good news is that, as netizens, our sense of being neglected by the people who would run the country— perhaps right into the ground—is not our paranoid imaginations in overdrive. They really aren't talking to us. Or about us.

The survey's most fascinating findings center on the youngest group—a category forming the heart of the digital world and the next generation of political leaders and voters.

Self-navigators are instantly recognizable to anyone who has spent any time online. They're behind much of the technology driving the development of the Net—and are increasingly running the show.

Although the political and journalistic establishment tends to dismiss them as civically apathetic, culturally inferior, or just plain stupid (self-navigators are known as Gen Xers in the media), they are potentially an enormously powerful political community—perhaps the most powerful—and certainly the broadest-based the world has seen. They are, for the most part, affluent, and have immediate access to much of the world's information. They have also developed the planet's most impressive and efficient communications system.

What is especially significant about these so-called self-navigators is their common ethos. They reject tradition and conformity. Only 3 percent say that "living by time-honored traditions" is always on their minds. Self-navigators share the values of their yuppie and post-yuppie elders (for instance, an emphasis on personal achievement), but they balance those values with a strong desire to maintain personal relationships, find security, and have fun.

Significantly, members of this group also believe they're responsible for their own welfare and well-being; they don't embrace the idea that government or some other entity should take care of them.

They are pragmatic. Many in the digital world believe that as technology becomes cheaper and easier to use—just as the phone, the tube, and the car did—everyone will eventually have access to it. Self-navigators don't necessarily feel responsible for seeing that everybody gets wired. This is a group that values competence and hard work. It is skeptical of social and civic safety nets. At the same time, security is more important to self-navigators than power, and close relationships are critical.

"Young people," write Chip Walker and Elissa Moses of the Brain Waves Group, "are building their own reliance networks with others who prove themselves trustworthy allies." Brain Waves found that self-navigators have concluded that the old formulas for success no longer apply. A college degree doesn't guarantee a job, and getting a job doesn't mean you'll keep it. Retirement may never be possible. Marriages can fail. Raising kids is insanely and increasingly expensive.

Yet self-navigators—in radical contrast to bleak boomer notions about the future—see the present as a time of great opportunity and are optimistic about their lives and prospects. "You can be a computer nerd like Bill Gates, or an overweight, emotionally stressed housewife like Roseanne, and still achieve success in your chosen field of endeavor," Walker and Moses point out.

The survey reinforces the outlines of the postindustrial, postpolitical ideology that has cropped up on countless Web sites and in online discussions. **Self-navigators embrace the Republican focus on individual rights but are wary of other values associated with the GOP.**

On the other hand, although this group's members celebrate diversity and tolerance—perhaps to a degree unprecedented in American politics—they don't believe that traditional liberal notions like welfare are feasible.

The individualism, tolerance, and rationality so prevalent on the Net contrast unmistakably with the exhausted ideologies during the 1996 campaign season—and with the equally dispirited and confused media struggling to render that battle meaningful.

MEET THE DIGITAL ELITE

It's a great irony of American cultural politics that so much of the clucking about the Internet centers on pornography and other dubious and unproven dangers to children. The profound moral crisis facing the Internet community is rarely mentioned, online or off.

The digital culture is fast becoming one of the most powerful and exclusive elites in history—one that becomes wealthier, better equipped, and more detached from poor, working-class Americans all the time. If you believe that money, information, and communications equal power—and history suggests strongly that they do—the digital elite will rule much of the world. And poor Americans will fall farther and farther behind.

In June 1996, the U.S. Census Bureau reported a growing gap between the richest and poorest Americans—the widest income disparity since the end of World War II. During the first two years of the Clinton administration, the share of national income earned by the top 5 percent of households grew at a faster rate than during the eight years of the Reagan administration.

According to the report, the factors contributing to the disparity are the shift away from the manufacturing jobs that paid high wages to relatively low-skilled workers, the decline of unions, increased reliance on computers and computer-assisted technology (which place a premium on skills and education), and the pervasive use of part-time workers.

The racial, social, and political consequences of this widening income gap are grave for the country as a whole, but the implications for the digital world are staggering.

Already, the online community is more affluent than the population at large. Computers, online services, and digital communications take time and money, not only for equipment, but for maintenance, telephone and transmission fees, and software.

If American families at the bottom are getting poorer, you don't have to be a social scientist to figure out they'll have even less of a chance to buy their way into the information era. Their kids, unable to pay phone and cable bills, will be barred from the educational and research facilities online. They will lack the ability to land the high-paying jobs that increasingly require computer literacy.

The founders of American democracy foresaw a culture in which citizens — white male citizens — had equal access to opportunity. Gradually, the ideal of equal opportunity has been expanded to include more and more segments of society. It's hard to square our political system's ideals of opportunity with the growing power clout of the digital elite.

Conventional political theory holds that once the poorer masses figure out that they aren't wired and that wealthy, employed Americans are, they'll explode and tear down the walls of the digital world. But how do you storm the Digital Nation, wired into millions of individual homes and offices?

A QUESTION OF MORALITY

Truly moral politicians — and moral digital citizens, for that matter — have a hummer of a problem on their hands: how to conceive and undertake a massive commitment to, and investment in, cheap technologies that would wire up the whole nation.

America has undertaken giant public works projects before: the Western expansion; the building of the railroads; the Tennessee Valley Authority, which brought electricity to rural America. It's neither unprecedented nor unimaginable.

It is, in fact, the single most pressing moral imperative of the Digital Age. Forget the fake — if popular — "moral" issues like decency, sexual orientation, violence on TV, and pornography. Every day, in magazines, newspapers, and on the tube, we see the consequences of our political system of the media elite — whose audience seems to shrink by the hour and whose relevance vanished years ago.

How this issue is dealt with — or not — will say a lot about whether America wants to face real, not imagined, issues of morality and whether the digital community is content to become just another entrenched media elite, soon to be despised by those legions outside the tent.

A QUESTION OF RESPONSIBILITY

My rants about the threat posed by a wealthy, educated digital elite, cut off from those masses who can't afford or don't want to use digital technology, always generate lots of mail that falls into four general categories:

1. It is the moral responsibility of the digital community to distribute technology and see that everyone gets to use it — not just a few.
2. It is up to individuals to decide whether they want to acquire this technology. The digital community has no responsibility to see that people outside join the community.
3. It is sophistry even to raise the issue of access. As happened with automobiles, TV, and radio, technology will inevitably make itself so cheap and readily available that anyone who wants to use it will be able to.
4. People are responsible for themselves. They can get wired if they really want to.

Net-thinking abhors traditional party labels and solutions, but borrows from various viewpoints.

Though netizens find the right wing clueless and rabid about things like morality, censorship, and family values, nearly all feel that liberals have failed to speak honestly about race, family, crime, and responsibility. It's almost as if the Digital Nation were especially wary of being sucked into such liberal traps as taking responsibility for large numbers of people whom they aren't sure want help — and whom they aren't sure they **can** help.

Many emailers and posters say they have witnessed the disasters of liberal ethics (like the welfare state) that have contributed to the existence of a vast underclass of people who take little responsibility for their own work lives or for the children they bring into the world. This kind of candor is common in email — as common as it is unheard-of in traditional media or national political discussions.

Netizens return again and again to the question of how to make society fair and tolerant. This is a goal they seem to enthusiastically embrace, while emphasizing — insisting —

that people who want help must assume more personal responsibility.

"It's very well-meaning," messaged a Harvard political science major about my call for government to distribute more computers, "but we know this won't work. We've seen it all our lives. It isn't that we don't care—that's a libel. It's that we don't mindlessly embrace solutions we know not only won't work, but are apt to create more problems, such as what to do with a million computers rotting and falling apart in underclass homes. We want a rational political agenda, not an unworkable ideological one."

Liberalism and conservatism have continually failed to address social issues effectively so that few people want to identify themselves as embracing either philosophy—and so far there isn't a name for the postpartisan philosophy that keeps bubbling up in the digital world.

In part, it is incredibly rational: You can't simply wire people up without first confronting much larger issues—family life, education, the economy. Computers require money, maintenance, and upgrading—and specific skills to use them. Just giving the machines to people suffering the social problems that are epidemic in our society would be silly.

In part, this view advances technology as an ideology unto itself: The evolving nature of technology will confront and solve these problems.

It is also Darwinian. The strong survive—the weak can't be saved.

TECHNOLOGY AND POLITICS

SHIFTING POWERS

Technology isn't just redefining politics in the Digital Nation. It's creating a whole new meaning of civics.

Historian Catherine Drinker Bowen called the 1787 Constitutional Convention the Miracle at Philadelphia. "Every miracle has its provenance," she wrote. "Every miracle has been prayed for." Bowen believed that great civic experiments were cause for celebration.

So it is with the digital world's coming of age. Of course, this community has grown too fast to figure out its political significance. Like a rider on a horse out of control, all most of us can do is to hang on and not get our heads knocked off by some low-hanging tree limb.

But we all sense something enormous happening around us. We are in the middle of a great experiment, which we, depending on help from others to keep us up to speed, can only try to follow one step at a time.

Technology is transforming democracy. It affects which political issues we consider, the speed at which they travel, the images through which we comprehend them, and the number of people who consider them. It also transforms the ways in which we interact with political leaders. In fact, it's changing who those leaders are.

Technology is as profoundly political as the stuff it transmits. "It all came from there," Lech Walesa once said, pointing to a TV when a reporter asked him why Communism fell.

But television, regulated and monopolized from the start, has been liberated by the new devices that have sprouted from it. The TV remote was, for a time, the most political gadget in America. It gave every person who used it new and sweeping control and changed a medium run by three greedy men for half a century. Cable television vastly increased viewers' choices. The same with the VCR, which made its many owners instant programming moguls.

The political impact of the zapper and the VCR, however, pales in comparison with that of the computer and the modem, which have given individuals more power over and more access to information, culture, media, and, potentially, politics than humans have ever had. This technology also raises important (if largely unanswered) questions about class, education, freedom, equality, privacy, technological hubris, and community.

The outside world still tends to define this new "power" in terms of whiz-bang gadgetry, its dazzling ability to move dirty pictures around, its handful of bomb instructors and militiamen, and the occasional ingenious hacker who drives some company or government agency buggy.

More interesting, though, is the way new technologies are altering politics.

Parents see power flow **from** them; they no longer have complete control over their children's cultural education. No wonder the mysteries of the Internet have sparked such anxiety, such a hue and cry from the elders.

Teachers find that their students have radically new ways of learning. Students have more access to information. Technology is changing our notions of literacy and teaching or education.

Journalists, whose monopoly on political reporting is waning, are forced, unhappily, to share the dissemination of news with raucous and opinionated loudmouths — us. Much to the dismay of professional pundits, we can participate in the political system again.

The eager moral guardians — so vocal in the 1996 presidential campaign — are distraught because they find it impossible to control the ideas they dislike. Those who struggle to enforce dogma and simplistic good-and-evil notions are loathe to find that their flocks have great freedom of information. We are free to escape imposed theology and to define our own spiritual lives. We can articulate our own values and morality.

The politicians see local, national, and global political communities—some increasingly powerful and influential—arising throughout the Digital Nation, independent of them and their control.

Even the police are feeling nervous about a world increasingly beyond their understanding. This, naturally, is why they argue for the ability to invade our privacy to a degree never before imagined.

Pat Buchanan and Bill Bennett don't know the half of it. There are enough power shifts in today's world for a score of cultural and political wars. Before we can comprehend the connection between technology and democracy, we need to grasp not how hip, cool, or new we are, or how impressive our toys are, but how intensely political and threatening this rising nation is to the media elite.

TECHNOLOGY AND COMMUNITY

Eerie cultural similarities exist between the emerging Digital Nation and the American colonies in the years before the Revolution.

Like the colonists, the Net community has a distinct sense of itself as a separate political entity. The digital community has transcended the idea that it is simply a new communications medium. It now has its own language, traditions, communities, values, culture, and political ethos.

Rulemakers will try to shape and control this new community—without grasping that it has no intention of acquiescing.

Just as England viewed the colonies as stupid, dangerous, and godless, the political and journalistic institutions view the digital world as filled with pornographers, weirdos, and hackers.

Much like the colonists who reveled in the Boston Tea Party, netizens couldn't curse enough online in the wake of the Communications Decency Act; they undermined the bill's authority and credibility while asserting their own.

We might as well call our governing body in Washington King George. The political and media establishments think they can tame and civilize the Net with laws promulgating decency and with bills regulating access. Washington doesn't yet comprehend that its attempt to impose its rules on this community is a doomed effort, breeding alienation, resentment, and defiance — not compliance.

THE TIMES SQUARE SYNDROME

Despite the sense of political identity that the CDA brought the Net, equally powerful forces are working to tame and sanitize the digital community. Not only to clean it up in the moral sense, but to make it safe for the real purpose of American media: turning a profit. Call it the Times Square Syndrome. It's not a new phenomenon — it's one of America's great and immutable historic forces.

The syndrome's name is inspired by the ongoing redevelopment of New York's Times Square district, known for years — in almost any media coverage of the area — as "seedy" Times Square. This part of midtown Manhattan is being redeveloped with a vengeance. Disney is renovating a theater. Time Warner is planning a vast Warner Brothers studio store. Giant office towers, hotels, and high-tech entertainment emporiums are on the boards and under construction.

The strippers, hookers, junkies, video-porn parlors, fortune-tellers, street rats, bodegas, boxing gyms, Greek burger joints, and gadget stores that characterized Times Square are almost all gone — closed, bought out, evicted, moved away.

The square is being made safe, prosperous, and wholesome again. Loads of money will be made as "decent" citizens flock to the sanitized neighborhood from all over the world.

If this drama is most familiar in the context of urban renewal, it's also a common syndrome in media. **Look at the history of newspapers and magazines, radio and TV — each medium started out raucous, idiosyncratic, sometimes**

vulgar and offensive. Each ended up tepid, conventional, and safe, once people figured out how to make money off the ventures.

Corporations buy great chunks of each medium and work with government — politicians and bureaucrats — to control access to and regulate every aspect of them. The corporations demand that media be made comfortable for families and "decent people," which necessitates some censorship and generates lots of noise about content. These companies tend to be powerful and politically plugged-in: Politicians listen to them intently.

TV, conceived by its inventors as a miraculously liberating, individualistic, and communal medium — all at the same time! — wasn't two years old before three companies owned it and the U.S. government tightly controlled and licensed it. Most magazines are now owned by vast media conglomerates and are indistinguishable from one another. Most papers are part of giant chains and are almost void of real opinion or distinct identity. They are obsessed with profits and are wedded to mass-market visions of what is news.

The Net and the Web are next in line for the Times Square Syndrome. The CDA was just the first salvo. In order for companies and their middle-class constituencies to thrive here, the Net must be seen as a safe environment. The digital equivalent of hookers, dealers, and porno vendors have to be cleared off the streets. Can't have little Johnny stumbling across dirty pictures, a Web site called **Suck,** or Jesus' homepage.

Another sign is the unmistakable wingbeat of billion-dollar vultures — Microsoft, AT&T, the Baby Bells — hovering around, trying to figure out how to control access and make money off Internet content. Compared to these rapacious beasts, CBS, NBC, and ABC look like wood nymphs.

In any other medium, the battle would already be over. But it isn't so simple on the Net. It might resist the Times Square Syndrome more vigorously than any medium ever has — at least enough to delay its inexorable conquest.

One reason is that there's still great confusion about which technology will work and in what ways. Will cable be the way in? Phone lines? Wireless? Microsoft is here, but it's far from clear that the digital behemoth is present in the right way, at the right place, or even at the right time. The company seems confused, flailing. In fact, Microsoft's editorial invasion of the Web might lead to the first major defeat in the company's quest for digital world domination.

Another obstacle is the relatively cheap and highly individualistic machinery of the digital world. With modems, computers, and phone lines, Net culture can form and re-form almost continuously. Unlike TV, radio, or any other medium scarfed up by suits, the Net already has an entrenched, highly outspoken, and fiercely independent culture in place.

Perhaps the Net is so vast and malleable that giant corporations and netizens can reside happily side by side. Of course, that would be like deer placidly grazing next to a velociraptor.

CELEBRATING INDIVIDUALITY

The trick for Net culture is to balance individuality and freedom with the need to unite as a political community, one that celebrates the idiosyncratic while engaging in civil political discourse.

If the Internet can escape Times Square Syndrome, if it can resist the inevitable onslaught of corporate greed, political interference, and government regulation, then it might actually show that technology can improve democracy rather than just taking pictures of it. It might allow for a bit of iconoclasm as well.

Mainstream media culture opposes such exploration and experimentation. Take the 1996 stories about Hillary Rodham Clinton and her White House meetings with psychologist and philosopher Jean Houston. They were completely lacking in imagination; they are thinly veiled reminders to public figures of just how perilous it is to stray from the shallow conventional thinking of the people who run America's newsrooms.

These stories have nothing to do with news, journalism, or politics and everything to do with misrepresenting the truth, mob journalism, and hype for Bob Woodward's new book.

Granted, Mrs. Clinton has worked hard to alienate the many people who were eager to support such an ethical-seeming, intelligent, and articulate woman in the White House. What a shame she didn't score a real blow for feminism by going out, landing a job, and doing something useful with her life and training rather than permitting her husband to make her "health care czar" or assuming the outdated, useless, impossible position of "first lady," a job as creepy as the term that describes it.

But she's done nothing to justify the stunning misrepresentations of her meetings with Houston, a motivational researcher and lecturer who holds advanced degrees in philosophy and religion; has taught at Columbia, Hunter College, and the University of California; has written books and articles; and who has worked for Unicef.

Dateline, CNN, the three networks, and major papers such as **The New York Times, The Washington Post,** and the **Los Angeles Times** all rushed crews and reporters to Pomona, New York, to confront Houston with reports—sparked by Bob Woodward's book, **The Choice** (Simon and Schuster, 1996)—that she encouraged Mrs. Clinton to have imaginary conversations with Eleanor Roosevelt and Mahatma Gandhi. Many media outlets used terms like **seance** and **New Age mysticism** to describe these meetings—terms that were not even used in Woodward's book.

Mrs. Clinton was made out to be a nut as well as a hustler and Houston a "New Age guru," a "psychic," a "spiritual advisor," or a person who engages in "transcendental psychobabble," depending on which media you watched or read. If Mrs. Clinton had met with a rabbi or Catholic priest, it wouldn't have been news at all—or it would have been reported as wholesome and in the best Judeo-Christian tradition. But because she had the temerity to meet with a serious scholar who works outside the traditional systems of belief, she's a kook.

So much for the media being charged with opening our minds instead of closing them.

"[Houston] has swum with dolphins, eaten worms at a Chinese banquet, chatted via sign language with chimpanzees, and lived with lepers in India," reported the **New York Daily News.** The connection was almost universally made between Mrs. Clinton's meetings with her and Nancy Reagan's much publicized — and equally exaggerated — meetings with an astrologer who supposedly dictated national policy.

In fact, Houston is not a mystic, guru, spiritualist, or faith healer. She's a motivational psychologist of the sort hired by scores of big companies, CEOs, athletes, and entertainers to help spark creativity, improve attitude, and focus thought. If anything, she's far better educated and respected than most. She advised Mrs. Clinton to imagine conversations with these famous women as an exercise, a method to help her focus on a book she was writing about children.

Mrs. Clinton has at least twice revealed her mental chats with Mrs. Roosevelt prior to the media flurry — once in her syndicated column, and once in a speech broadcast via cable. One oddity did emerge in the ensuing talking-head discussions: Middle-aged white men — Robert Novak, Orrin Hatch — thought such conversations were "loopy" or "weird," but women — Susan Estrich, Geraldine Ferraro — said they often had mental dialogues with their dead parents, siblings, or friends; that it was a way of staying in touch with people they'd lost and was helpful to them in their work and personal lives.

The message of the mainstream media is clear: Only dull, conventional, and safe personal behavior is acceptable from public figures. **Any kind of unconventional sexual, spiritual, or personal exploration, any self-doubt or intellectual inquiry will be ridiculed, distorted, and used against you.**

Only the Ronald Reagans of the world — people who profess (often hypocritically) Hollywood definitions of morality and probity — can possibly survive.

Mass media has, especially in modern times, crowded out individual voices. We can't broadcast our own TV shows or publish our own newspapers.

But any geek with a modest wad of money can be an online publisher in a flash, by creating his or her own Web page or computer conferencing system. Most of these new creations are interactive, and they welcome input.

This technology, more accessible than existing media technologies, has fostered a riotous explosion of individual voices even as mainstream media focus more and more on powerful elites with a lens that grows increasingly narrow.

Granted, the Net is frequently chaotic and confusing. But online, diversity and nonconformity are realities of everyday life. Pluralism—in journalism, in politics, in society—can stage an overdue comeback.

POSTPUNDITRY

POSTPOLITICS

POSTPOP

A NEW CIVICS

DEMOCRACY'S DISCONTENT

Except for Washington reporters and politicians, nobody is happy about the nation's fragmented, abrasive, and superficial politics or the paucity of choices it offers us these days. It's hard to know which of the competing visions is worse: the hostility toward the weak, the heartless phobias and intrusive moral crusades of the right, or the bankrupt ideology and fuzzy-headed myopia of the left.

Our public life is rife with discontent, writes Harvard professor Michael J. Sandel in his 1996 book, **Democracy's Discontent: America in Search of a Public Philosophy** (Harvard University Press): "Americans do not believe they have much say in how they are governed and do not trust government to do the right thing."

The political parties, says Sandel, are unable to make sense of our condition. Neither, he might have added, are our political journalists.

Sandel identifies the unhappiness (evident in just about every online political discussion group and TV talk show) most of us feel about the seemingly shattered civic process.

At the heart of the discontent, he writes, are two concerns: The fear that we are losing control of the forces that govern our lives and the sense that the moral fabric of our community is unraveling around us. This anxiety is a deepening condition that both major parties have failed to address in their political agendas.

Disenchantment with democracy has always been a striking—if indirect—theme of the online world. An outsider culture to begin with, the digital world has instinctively rejected (as Sandel does in his book) extreme conservatism and knee-jerk liberalism as inviable political ideologies incapable of solving social problems.

"The global media and markets that shape our lives beckon

us to a world beyond boundaries and belonging," writes Sandel. "But the civic resources we need to master these forces, or at least to contend with them, are still to be found in the places and stories, memories and meanings, incidents and identities, that situate us in the world and give our lives their moral particularity."

To restore faith, he argues, we need to revive a sense of moral purpose in our civic life, which has become fragmented and unmanageable. We don't need one world community, but many smaller communities and political bodies. **The nation-state doesn't have to vanish, only cede its claim as the sole repository of power and the primary focus of our political allegiance.**

In the contemporary world, Sandel writes, nation-states are losing the allegiance of their citizens—typically based on sovereignty and collective allegiance identity.

Nations are being eroded from above by the integration of world financial markets, the global nature of industrial production, and the movement of capital, goods, and information across national boundaries. At the same time, they are challenged from below by the resurgence of subnational groups for autonomy and self-rule.

As their effective sovereignty fades, says Sandel, nation-states are losing much of their hold on their citizens. (This makes a lot of sense—much more than most of what we've heard in the political campaign—and helps put in context the ennui that surrounds America's civic life.)

Sandel predicts: "Even the most powerful states cannot escape the imperatives of the global economy; even the smallest are too heterogeneous to give full expression to the communal identity of any one ethnic or national or religious group without oppressing others who live in their midst."

So what, then? Sandel suggests reshaping the boundaries and the size of nations—forming smaller communities and entities.

The kinds of entities Sandel envisions sound eerily like the diverse and outspoken communities of the Digital Nation — where citizens are comparatively loyal to their civics and are struggling to form a coherent and rational political ideology for their new world. The online world is still rooted in traditions of invention, discovery, and free thought — notions that are easy to feel good about.

Communities in the "real" world, on the other hand, had quite a bit less to be sanguine about as they — we — recovered from the 1996 political season — yet another that reduced our political life to its lowest common denominators: sound bites, negative advertising, money, mean-spiritedness, and fragmentation.

The primary question facing us isn't about who raised the gasoline tax three years ago or who is to blame for escalating prices, but exactly what our country, one presidential term short of the millennium, **is** anymore.

THE TECHNOCRACY

The New Atlantis, one of the first works to envision a technocracy, was never completed. Its author, Francis Bacon, an essayist of the late sixteenth and early seventeenth centuries, died forty pages into it.

As he looks down from philosopher heaven onto the evolving cyberscape below, Bacon must be wishing he could finish his now timely work.

Nobody is exactly sure what conclusions Bacon would have reached in **The New Atlantis.** Some historians — like political scientist Langdon Winner — believe he wanted to develop his idea that the political world was corrupt and inefficient while the scientific and technological one was pure, intelligent, and competent.

This notion is the core ideology of many of the Net's most passionate advocates. They believe that a powerful subculture is developing exclusive knowledge about how to pull the levers that control things. (Of course, this is a core **fear** of Net resistors.)

Bacon had played around with utopian visions in earlier writings. A fervent advocate of science and technology, he believed that the world inevitably would be ruled by scientists and technicians—those who had access to the machines, information, and skills necessary to gather pertinent, accurate information and solve complex problems.

But Bacon and most other utopians understood the inherent tragedy of such a society: great masses of humanity would be excluded from the political and technical elite that governed them. In Bacon's time, of course, disenfranchised masses were the rule—in fact, their exclusion from power was the reigning reality in the world.

As science and technology became more complex, Bacon's theory asserted, the elite—the Technocracy—would become more and more powerful. Most people would fall further and further behind. This, many visionaries and utopians of that time believed, was a historical inevitability.

In America, though, high-end media have long been an elite. Poor people don't listen to NPR or line up to buy **The New Yorker, The New Republic,** or even **The Los Angeles Times.**

But a technocracy is taking distinct shape in this country—especially when the term is applied to the educated and affluent assortment of academics, politicians, bureaucrats, kids, programmers, artists, writers, engineers, and other netizens who make up the digital culture.

None of them set out to be an elite or to exclude large numbers of people from their new world, but all of them will have to live with that specter. Online citizens already have access to tons of information other people don't have access to and they have access as well to what is perhaps the Technocracy's most powerful resource — one another.

As machines become more pervasive and more sophisticated, the new Technocracy is taking shape, whether we mean it to or not. And we can see Bacon's foreboding vision about the Technocracy taking shape, too—because lots of our fellow citizens aren't in it.

It's hard to imagine a question that will have more impact on politics, the economy, education, class, media, and civic discourse than the distribution of this new technology.

A 1995 study by the U.S. Commerce Department's National Telecommunications and Information Administration found that only 4.5 percent of poor, rural households own computers, compared with 7.6 percent for innercity homes and 8.1 percent for the urban-area poor.

In contrast, nearly a third of middle-class households in America have computers.

A 1995 NAACP study found that while the number of black college students using computers and Web sites is growing, the gap between black and white children is widening. A University of Texas study that same year found that Latinos are far less likely than whites to have access to computers at school, work, or home and that this disparity is also increasing. More than a third of whites and Asians, in contrast, have computers at home or work.

America was founded on the opposite idea, however, and the concept of permanently disenfranchised peoples in this country is explosively unacceptable, on the Net or off. At the heart of American politics is the idea that everybody can—and should—be included.

Hundreds of years after these American ideals were first tossed around, new developments, digital and otherwise, have taken this momentous topic—the distribution and availability of technology and of knowledge—and made it one of the central political and moral issues of the modern world.

NEW RATIONALISM

Rationalism was a smaller cousin of the Enlightenment. Writers such as John Locke, Jonathan Swift, and later, Thomas Paine and Thomas Jefferson, preached a version of rationalism in the eighteenth century. The Web could make rationalism a global twenty-first-century political ideology.

Existing ideologies and institutions—liberalism, conservatism, worship of God, journalism—are largely irrational. They fail to address issues such as race, poverty, economics, welfare, family, and education with factual clarity and reliability. Examples of irrationality include:

• Most Americans believe violence comes from TV though it doesn't.
• Many blacks believe police brutality is worsening though it isn't.
• Many whites believe blacks prefer taking welfare to working though they don't.
• Many parents claim the Internet is dangerous though it isn't.
• Many gun owners believe the Constitution guarantees their right to buy machine guns though it doesn't.
• Some religious people believe gay teachers are likely to molest their students though they aren't.

In a cover story titled "The Last Taboo" in the October 14, 1996, **New Republic,** iconoclastic columnist Wendy Kaminer argues that one problem in American politics is that there's too much—not too little—belief in God.

Kaminer argues that H. L. Mencken (who once wrote that religion is so "absurd that it comes close to imbecility") would be amazed by contemporary public policy discussions, suffused as they are with piety. "The rise of virtue talk—which generally takes the form of communitarianism on the left and nostalgia for Victorianism on the right— has resulted in a striking remoralization of public policy debates," Kaminer writes.

Religion is often at odds with rationality. Almost all Americans—95 percent—profess some belief in God, and a 1994 survey by US News & World Report found 76 percent imagine God as a heavenly father who pays attention to their prayers. Meanwhile, Gallup reports that 44 percent believe in the biblical account of creation, and 36 percent of all Americans describe themselves as born-again. At the same time, 53 percent of Catholics and 40 percent of Protestants profess belief in UFOs. About one-quarter of Americans have faith in astrology. Nearly one-third of American teenagers believe in reincarnation.

These statistics are ironic, to say the least. We have so much data at our fingertips, yet so many of us cling to beliefs rather than embrace fact, rationality, and skepticism.

People need those beliefs, spiritual or otherwise. As Kaminer suggests, Americans are given few other alternatives, especially in the media and in their political lives. Contemporary media don't kick around the notion of whether God exists. But such conversations take place online everyday. Might they move us, over time, to choose rationalism over dogma?

In the October 1996 issue of **MIT Technology Review**, senior editor Herb Brody writes on how the digital world is transforming science and research: "The Internet—fruit of science past—is nourishing today's research enterprise by fostering collaboration and speeding the distribution of new data."

The dissemination, absorption, and sharing of research is faster and simpler with the Net. Libraries that have only a few computers can access the Internet, isolated researchers can share their colleagues' works, and experts can provide almost immediate feedback to inquiries.

This suggests the possibility of a rational political culture in which decisions are informed not by the gaseous, hypocritical, and pious rhetoric of politics and journalism, but by factual information shared instantly—for the first time in history—with the rest of the world.

Rationalism could educate new generations in reality rather than rhetoric and force the rest of us—with relentless doses of truth—to confront our own ill-formed and unsupported beliefs.

Over time, the distribution of facts can change the stalemated way our media confront politics. This process could elevate truth over faith, rationality over rhetoric, and fact over argument.

HIVE OF REASON

From the responses I received to my ideas about rationalism, it was clear that I'd pushed a button. Pro or con,
webheads appear nearly starved for the chance to take a
whack at stuff like this.

Wearied by years of reading clunky Net-as-utopia dis-
courses from cybergurus and digital cheerleaders, some
readers slammed the suggestion that the Net fosters
more rational debate than the forums that have come
before it.

"Oh, not more Net-will-save-the-world talk," was one
message. **"The Net is pure chaos," read another. "How could
any ideology of rationalism grow and prosper here?"**

Many others agreed that American civic discussions had
become irrational, obsessed with God, and overpowered
by cheap values and the suffocating dogma of ideologies
like liberalism and conservatism.

As counterpoint to the naysayers, researchers for whom
the Net is nothing less than a miracle wrote me. The Net
is increasing by extraordinary leaps the speed and quality
of the information they can receive. I heard from British,
German, and Dutch graduate students and teachers whose
lives have been literally and figuratively transformed by
the Net.

"You're onto something, I think. The Net has great
potential in creating a new rationalism," emailed a political
science professor at Tufts. "Debunking is very possible
online, especially debunking of irrational ideologies at odds
with research and reality. These ideologies totally dominate American politics."

"We are ripe for a new Rationalism," wrote a graduate
student of philosophy at Harvard. "The truth is, most of
our positions on politics are illogical. But the first Enlightenment was about discovery. This one would have to be
about reason."

There were also poignant messages from disenchanted
digital pioneers who see the Net as increasingly brutal,

contentious, chaotic, and corporatized. "I won't live to see a rational Web," wrote one retired hacker.

The nature of the Net does foster rationality. Ideas must meet an especially high standard. In mainstream media, ideas are relegated to op-ed pages where the audience is generally small, the life span is one morning, and response is almost impossible.

The intense sifting of ideas, facts, and information on the Web counters dogma and prejudice in favor of truth. **Time**'s infamous "Cyberporn" cover story would never have been so soundly and rapidly debunked in the days before the Web, which gave researchers, journalists, and others a chance to gather accurate information quickly and share it immediately. Thus, an irrational notion — that the Web is overrun by pornographers and perverts — was immediately challenged and corrected.

As anyone who's spent time on the Web knows, this is not the medium for dumb or unsupported notions. Unlike in other media, smart people can get at you quickly and in great numbers. They can also teach you, and are surprisingly generous about taking the time to do so.

The dissemination of ideas on the Web is such that any given idea passes through many minds. Like bees leaving a hive, they circle the world, picking up corrections, amplifications, criticisms, and support. They are recycled through countless Web sites and newsgroups. They either capture the imagination or they don't. The ultimate test of an idea on the Net isn't whether the author can out-debate the idea's critics, but whether the idea can take on a life of its own, passing out of the hive and across a world whose boundaries seem to have mysteriously vanished.

Sometimes the idea never comes back — it vanishes into the ether. Sometimes it comes back bloody, but unbowed. It never comes back precisely as it left.

POSTPU

POSTP

POSTPO

MAY I INTRODUCE MYSELF?

Maybe it's the piercing blue eyes. Maybe it's the matching PowerBooks. People are comparing me to Tom Cruise.

Of course, there's the reckless derring-do and hand-eye co-ordination Tom exhibited in **Top Gun,** so reminiscent of my own driving habits. It could also be the way his courageous, tenacious courtroom style in **A Few Good Men** echoes the way I argue with my wife.

Tom and I both take risks...from time to time.

So, as soon as it was released, my daughter and I rushed to see **Mission: Impossible** at the Sony Theaters gigaplex in Wayne, New Jersey (home of Digital Surround Stereo Sound, fresh pretzel bites, and the renowned popcorn-soda combo). We had a superior vantage point: just twenty-five feet from the two-story screen.

It was there—despite my hearty recommendation of this movie—that I was struck by at least one profound differ-ence between Tom Cruise and me: our digital lives.

Granted, we both use our PowerBooks a lot, but the similarities end there—as my jeering daughter repeatedly pointed out. I was so struck by this during the movie that I decided to go home and compare my computer experiences with his. I jotted down a few notes, first in the dark theater and then later as I tried to log on to HotWired.

I can't be all that precise about this, because I couldn't really decipher any of the notes I wrote in the dark, but the first digital dissonance between Tom's life and mine appears when Secret Agent Ethan Hunt staggers from a spectacular near-death experience to a safe house, goes straight for the PowerBook sitting on a table, and logs on to the Net in something like four seconds.

In another eight seconds, he breaks a complex code involving a passage from the Book of Job and sends a message to an international arms dealer named Max. When he slips a disk into his machine, the computer reads it in nanoseconds. Two minutes later, the secret arms dealer responds and agrees to set up a meeting for the next day.

I got back from the movie around eleven, and it took me four minutes just to open the laptop case—a polyester thread got stuck in the zipper—then to plug in my own PowerBook, stick the phone jack in, and wait for it to finish loading. It took another ninety seconds to attach the dock.

Maybe I'm using the wrong disks, but mine take nearly a minute to load. Tom's machine scarfs up graphics instantly, practically vacuuming them, while mine harbors enmity toward anything other than text and resists accordingly.

Tom's PowerBook always seems to load instantly. No smiling Mac face, no extensions popping up deliberately, and no MacOS loading bar—which is just as well, because the seconds lost waiting for those little treats could easily mean the end for Tom, the MI Strike Force, indeed the entire Free World.

I decided to try AOL's new Netscape Web browser first. It took four minutes before AOL told me I couldn't log on because my modem hadn't connected and to try again later. Then I got a message saying it was busy.

Here, Cruise and I part company. He is intense and would have blown a fuse. I remained cool as ice. I activated my Config PPP, but the line was busy, so I sat for three minutes listening to the automatic redial, which makes my dogs crazy—they think it's an intruder and start barking.

The time lag for Tom in the movie would have been bad enough, but any barking dogs would surely have ruined his mission and gotten him killed.

The Config PPP dialed for five minutes. We were now pushing twenty-one minutes, and I hadn't even gotten online, let alone logged on to The Netizen. The dogs were still barking, so my wife yelled at me to shut them up, and I skirted all these wires and lines sticking out all over the place. Ah, but for Tom's machine, which seems to float, serenely unencumbered, over the table.

Finally, the modem handshake was completed. I made it to Netscape, where it took forty-five seconds for the home-page to load, then to the HotWired menu, where I sat for another minute while all those graphics tried to squeeze through my teeny phone line. I went to Threads on The Netizen, where it took two minutes to load the graphics and text. Then my modem clicked distressingly, and the number of blinking lights went suddenly from seven to two.

Two more minutes passed before a message came up saying the server was refusing to accept Netscape. I got right back on the horse, as it were, and did it all again. But I neglected to disconnect the Config PPP, so it took several more minutes (I forgot to time this mishap, maybe because it happens so often) before I figured it out and tried to get back on AOL, which had to reset my modem three times. As far as I could tell, Tom never even had to set his modem, much less reset it.

This time, it took only four minutes to log on to the Net, get on to HotWired, to The Netizen, and finally to Threads. Of course, everyone on my strike force would have been dead by this point and the arms dealers would have been long gone, but something even more menacing awaited me: pissed off **Wired** editors swarming like displaced hornets, trashing me for rants that I wrote about the magazine that appeared in this space. Again, I remained stone cool.

Cruise and his buddies use their laptops to penetrate top-secret files, track people walking through the CIA's offices, listen to noises, and monitor heat levels. They duel with machines nestled in the laps of evildoers; they insert false information into their email messages and block modems from transmitting diabolical schemes. Courageous, stub-born, and inventive laptops battle more frequently in the movie than Cruise does.

At one point, Cruise downloads tons of top-secret information from the CIA in less time than it takes me to get on to AOL.

Then there's that last—and infuriating!—difference between Tom's sublime email and my prosaic equivalent: his whizzes across his screen in swirling envelopes. Mine stacks up in ugly little lines, filled with codes, routing information, and numbers I don't understand.

Is Tom mocking me?

GENERATION X-FILES

MANIFESTO

Children are at the epicenter of the information revolution,
ground zero of the digital world. They will continue to build
it, and they understand it better than anyone. Not only is
the digital world making the young more sophisticated by
altering their ideas of culture and literacy, it is connecting
them to one another and providing them with a new sense
of political self. **Children are occupying a new kind of cultural
space; they represent the first generation for whom politics,
culture, and media are one.**

After centuries of sometimes benign, other times brutal oppres-
sion, kids are moving out from under our pious control,
finding one another via the great hive that is the Net. As
digital communications burst through the most heavily
fortified borders and ricochet around the world free from
governments and censors, so can children for the first time
reach past the suffocating boundaries of social convention,
past their elders' rigid notions of what is good for them.
No longer will children be seen and not heard; they will be
seen and heard more than ever.

And yet many choose to ignore this shift, hewing to the
notion that the young **must** remain under the control of
others, the last significant social entity in America to
remain indentured.

Because society has moved to protect kids against exploitation
and physical abuse, in the next century kids will make up
the only group in our so-called democracy with no inherent
political rights, no voice in the political process. Teenagers
in particular can be subjected to intolerable controls over
almost every aspect of their lives.

In part, it's that fears for children are manifold, ranging from
real danger (assault, molestation, kidnapping) to such
perceived—but often unprovable—perils as damage caused
by violent or pornographic imagery, the addictive nature

of some new technology, supposed loss of civilization and culture. In some segments of America, these fears seem valid. But for middle-class families that consume much of this controversial popular culture, such fears seem misplaced and exaggerated. They are invoked mostly to regain control of a society changing faster than our ability to comprehend it.

The need to protect children is instinctive. Letting them wander beyond our rigid boundaries, control may be the bitterest pill for many to swallow.

Under their guardians' noses, the young are now linked all over the world. They already share a culture online, trading information about new movies, TV shows, and CDs; warning one another about viruses; sharing software and tech tips. At times, they band together to chastise or drive out aggressive, obnoxious, or irresponsible digital peers. They steer one another to Web sites that interest them.

Despite such beneficial habits, children are being subjected to an intense wave of censorship—what with blocking software, V-chips, and ratings systems on everything from movies to computer games. Cultural conservatives want to put cultural blinders on the young. Political moderates embrace the idea that parents should have the right to block kids' TV programs. Social liberals have left kids up to their own devices and offer little support or defense.

That's why the notion that all children possess some basic rights is critical. Their choices should not be left to the arbitrary and ignorant whims of educators, religious leaders, or parents any more than people ought to be subject to the total control of monarchs. Parents who thoughtlessly ban access to lyrics or to online culture they don't understand, or who exaggerate the threat of violent imagery, are acting out of their own anxiety and arrogance. Rather than preparing kids for the world they will live in, these parents insist on preparing them for a world that no longer exists.

The idea that a TV show or song lyric can transform a healthy, grounded child into a dangerous monster is absurd, an irrational affront not only to science but to common sense. It is the invention of politicians (who use it to frighten or rally supporters), of powerful religious leaders (who can't teach dogma to the young without control), and of journalists (who see new media and culture as menaces to their once-powerful and highly profitable position in American society).

The idea that parents and guardians would even **want** to block kids' access to any topic is an affront to the ethos of the digital community. Some blocking software would screen out the poet Anne Sexton because her last name contains the word **sex.** V-chips could block out **Schindler's List** because people are killed in it. Parents might screen opposing political or cultural points of view — about atheism, abortion, pacifism — from their kids' computers or TVs.

As powerful as they are, media and culture — or the sometimes offensive imagery transmitted by them — can't form our children's value systems or their conscience. Only we can do that. Blocking, censoring, and banning should be our **last** resort in dealing with children, not our first.

Rational adults must accept that censorship and arbitrary controls don't work; they must realize that they have to thrash out a shared value system with their children. Most older kids can circumvent almost all censorious technology anyway, and since much of the digital world is beyond the comprehension of most parents, authority becomes meaningless. Children will learn not how to form value systems, but how their moral guardians can't make dictums stick.

For their part, children should spell out what they want to access: which TV shows, which CDs, how much time online. And they must specify what they're willing to do in exchange. They must agree to follow rules of safety: to not give out telephone numbers or home addresses to strangers online, and to tell parents about any pornography they come across. Media access is granted as a right, but it's subject to some conditions.

Families need to rely on trust, negotiation, and communication, not phobias, conflict, or suspicion.

It's imperative that children get their hands on the new machines. They need equal access to the technology of culture, research, and education. The machinery gives them media and culture—it's their universal language. Technology is their ticket to modern literacy, which in the next millennium will be defined as the ability to **find** information, rather than **regurgitate** it.

If new technology can create a gap between haves and have-nots, it can also narrow it. Cheap, portable PCTVs—televisions with computers and cable modems—will help equalize the digital revolution in a hurry. Hastening their arrival should be the most pressing moral issue of the digital generation.

Children need help in becoming civic-minded citizens of the digital age, in figuring out how to use the machinery for some broader social purpose than simple entertainment. They need our **guidance** in managing their new ability to connect instantly with other cultures, but they don't need our **parental despotism.**

It's time to extend to children the promise that John Locke introduced to the world three centuries ago: That everyone has rights. That everyone should be given as great a measure of freedom as possible. That all should have the opportunity to rise to the limits of their potential.

The approaching millennium gives children a chance to reinvent communications, culture, and community. Instead of holding them back, we should be pushing them forward. Instead of shielding them, we should take them by the hands, guide them to the gates, and cheer them on.

MISCONCEPTIONS

Children spend more time watching TV and going online and less time playing sports, exercising, or yucking it up with in-the-flesh companions than they did a decade ago.

Or so says mainstream journalism, which for decades has advanced the notion that our children are addicted to and endangered by the violent, stupid, and pornographic things they see on television and, more recently, on the computer screen.

This vision of sluggish, disconnected, brain-damaged, pornography-bombarded, Beavis-and-Butt-head-corrupted children predominates in American journalism. It has become a common theme of our political discourse as well. William Bennett makes millions off it. Bob Dole made it a central theme of his campaign. Boomer parents are convinced of it. The V-chip was approved partially in response to it. Few teachers would dispute it. The CDA was passed, in part, because of it.

Our kids, we're told, are getting dumber, lazier, and less moral because of what they see on the screen.

What a jaw-dropper it was to see this paragraph buried deep in an April 1996 **New York Times** story about how today's kids are actually spending their days:

"Many children spend more time than they did a decade ago in weekend and after-school sports or other activities, according to a Nickelodeon/Yankelovich study released last November."

Talk about burying a lead! For years, the war against children and their culture has been predicated on the idea that the new, mostly screen-driven media machinery draws kids more and more deeply into a sort of hypnotic vegetative state while their colleagues in other, more "disciplined" countries are doing push-ups and learning calculus.

But if kids are more active now than they were ten years ago—even though today there are so many more things to watch on TV or do online—something is profoundly wrong with the picture media have been painting.

Without question, certain kids in certain areas—especially among the underclass—are too often left alone with the TV.

But middle-class children, the pride and joy of the anxious boomers, seem to be on the soccer field in greater numbers than ever. They're interacting with their friends, getting the blood circulating in the fresh air, well away from their modems and TV remotes.

Journalism has distorted (and attacked) kid culture ever since comics and rock 'n' roll. **The media are already paying dearly for their long and relentless war on kids: They don't have any young customers left.** But the notion that popular culture is turning our children into degenerates is still one of the most enduring falsehoods in the country.

MORE MISCONCEPTIONS

I find myself already falling into a dangerous trap: I'm generalizing about kids without defining whom I'm talking about. Who are our kids? When do they become adults? These are not just semantic questions.

The May 1996 issue of **American Demographics** magazine reported that more than one-fifth of twenty-five-year-olds in the United States live with one or both parents and that the number is growing: In 1970 it was 15 percent. Young adults are waiting longer than their parents did to venture out of the nest, and those who do leave—to get married, join the army, go to school—are not necessarily gone for good.

Traditional temporal markers of adulthood are shifting. In 1970, the median age for women at first marriage was 20.8, almost a record low for the century. For men, it was 23.2. In 1994, the median age at first marriage was 24.5 for women and 26.7 for men, according to the Census Bureau. The median age of first-time mothers has also increased—from 22 in 1970 to 24 in 1993, according to the National Center for Health Statistics.

The line between kids and adults may have started blurring in the Vietnam War era, when citizens eighteen and older were granted the right to vote. Many teenagers have sex, live together, even get married before they can watch NC-17 movies legally.

Symbols of adulthood that once seemed clear—marriage, kids, careers, home ownership—are disappearing. By these standards, the young may never be considered adults. With such traditional mileposts becoming increasingly out of reach, many young people can postpone indefinitely the transition from "youth" to "adulthood."

So what? Well, a primary reason for the CDA was to "protect the young." It's also the reason for the V-chip and blocking software. But if we no longer have a consensus on who the young are, how can we understand these cultural conflicts and concerns?

When exactly do the young no longer need protection? When are they entitled to their own membership on AOL and the right to access newsgroups and the Web? To punch in credit card numbers for purchases?

Are those under twelve our only children, even as millions of people in their twenties have yet to become adults by conventional standards?

The digital generation will continue to foil our attempts to define, to protect, to condescend. AOL handles mask age as well as race and gender. Threads asks you for a log on and then lets you rip. It will become increasingly farcical to insist on the already arbitrary divisions between people — in the interest of protecting some of us from others.

Mike A. Males has written a meticulously researched and utterly convincing book called **The Scapegoat Generation: America's War on Adolescents** (Common Courage Press, 1996). It should be rammed down the throat of every venal politician and blockhead reporter who passes along certain myths about the young—TV and gangsta rap cause violence; teenagers are sexually irresponsible; welfare programs promote teen pregnancy; teen suicide and drug use are epidemic.

The real scandal involving America's youth, argues Males, is that while adult America is getting wealthier, the United States has the highest rate of child poverty of any Western nation.

The problems facing children have little to do with media, culture, sexuality, or permissiveness. In the United States, sixteen million children and teens live in poverty. It's not surprising that violent youth crime has risen rapidly —

murder is up 50 percent since the last decade, and violent crime arrests have doubled.

Knee-jerk adult outrage about the decline of the young ignores the stark reality that race, class, gender, and geography are far greater predictors of violence than, say, music.

Males points out that although public officials are quick to blame violent media for rising murder rates among the young, they rarely point out that in rural and suburban areas, the murder rate for kids is almost nonexistent, even though the same dread media that blares out of boom boxes in underclass tenements pours out of stereos in ranches and split-levels.

Scapegoat Generation should be hidden in backpacks and lunch boxes, posted on Web sites, and stuffed inside Bill Bennett's hoary books of moral tales. **Someone** needs to know the truth.

GENERATION X-FILES

America's most political TV show has yet to catch the attention of the many would-be censors and moral guardians eager to slow our children's plunge into digital and cultural hell.

The program is the defiant antithesis of Bennett's blockhead parables for children, Dole's nineteenth-century take on culture, and Clinton's creepy embrace of the useless V-chip (which will certainly be used to try to block The X-Files—good luck!). And to Buchanan, The X-Files would surely be the electronic Antichrist.

Beneath the veil of aliens, fat-sucking serial killers, sewer people, lepers, mutants, lava dwellers, and robotic cockroaches from outer space, **The X-Files** is the perfect reflection of the postpolitical generation's attitudes toward government, science, culture, and authority. As deliciously subversive as it is inventive, strange, and captivating, **The X-Files is one of the most intelligent and vehemently anti-government programs ever to appear over commercial airwaves.**

Its heroes—FBI agents Fox Mulder and Dana Scully—are ideal warriors of the digital generation. They're smart as rats, nonideological, deeply mistrustful of government. Their lives are enmeshed in new media and technology—from the dirty videos and sci-fi movies Mulder watches in his dingy apartment, to the cell phones the two use constantly to call each other, to the computers they use to record their haunting journals, tap into alien databases, and research crimes of assorted repulsives.

Mulder relies heavily on three wizard hackers who form the editorial staff of a conspiracy-oriented magazine called **The Lone Gunman,** and who function as a sort of digital think tank. They are wonderful creations, instantly familiar to anyone who has ever gone to a hacker gathering.

Scully is a woman of the '90s—fearlessly equal, compassionate, and ethical. She shares Mulder's suspicions about authority but, unlike Mulder, clings to the tenets of science over the laws of the supernatural. The eternal debate about technology and spirituality that has powered many of the world's great myths—from Frankenstein to Dr. Jekyll and Mr. Hyde—is played out in the continuous tension between the two agents.

The motto of **The X-Files** is The Truth Is Out There, but its intent is to show that one of government's primary functions is to keep anybody from learning it. Motives are always murky, as are the lines between black and white, good and evil.

Generation X-Files grew up with few real heroes or leaders. The idea that politicians lie and journalists aren't much better is no longer a controversial notion among the young; it is a given—at the crux of their political lives.

This generation has grown up picking and sorting through information, in a search for truth the way bag ladies look for cans—all amid waves of hype, spin, "objectivity," and hypocrisy, from eternally warring spokespeople and self-interested ideologues. Liberals and conservatives—along with permanently perplexed boomer parents—have failed this generation miserably.

Although elders continually try to shield the young from technology, the young have learned—like Scully and Mulder—to use it as a comparatively safe and honest way to find community.

Like many of their viewers, Mulder and Scully aren't apathetic, hardened, or embittered by all their troubles. On the contrary, they are idealists. They believe that the truth is out there and that trying to find it is worth any risk.

POSTPUNDITRY

POSTPOLITICS

POSTPOP

MY FAVORITE MEGALOMANIACS

WHERE IS MENCKEN WHEN WE REALLY NEED HIM?

The politicians who preach morals to Americans, wrote H. L. Mencken in 1926, tend to be fanatics, not statesmen. Mencken lived to roast censorious politicians, especially the value-spouting sort.

Boy, could we use some Mencken these days.

He would have drooled over William Bennett's transition from failed bureaucrat to modern-day moral crusader. He would have spotted in a second that the undermining of freedom in the name of morality is the fastest growing political movement of our time.

Among the few absolute articles of faith to which Mencken subscribed was this: When politicians start talking morality, grab your wallet and your children and run for your life.

William "Book of Virtues" Bennett has ridden the morals-and-culture horse to the max. He's become a multimillionaire from peddling expensive books of parables for children. After reviewing movies with Bob Dole in the presidential election campaign, he became the king of the talk show circuit. He is codirector of a group called Empower America and is said by political writers to be possibly jockeying for a spot in the 2000 presidential race.

Edgar Bronfman, CEO of MCA, actually flew to Washington in 1996 to assure Bennett that MCA-owned Interscope Records—the label Bennett pressured Time Warner into selling last year—would put its albums through a "comprehensive review process" to guard against offensive content. (The entertainment conglomerate is now owned by Bronfman's Seagram Company.)

But two of Interscope's best-selling rap albums, **Tha Doggfather** by Snoop Doggy Dogg and **The Don Killuminati: The 7 Day Theory** by Tupac Shakur (recorded under the name Makaveli) don't meet Bennett's standards of wholesome entertainment. He claims they glorify violence and degrade women.

"When I saw this stuff," Bennett huffed to the **Times** about Bronfman, "I thought, 'He did not keep his word.'"

Here is a Menckenesque spectacle if ever there was one: The heir to a liquor fortune and the architect of America's failed drug and education policies slug it out over what kind of music should be created and sold.

This issue of children's culture has become so loopy that all our conventional political wires seem to have crossed. We're in a kind of social meltdown, our rationality swept away by rhetoric and mesmerizing values-talk journalism.

Boomers who once thought themselves revolutionaries are rushing to endorse ratings systems, the V-chip, and blocking software to sanitize their kids' experiences. People who call themselves conservatives are happy to give giant corporations the right to make their cultural and moral choices for them. Liberals obsessed with free speech are glad to snatch it from rappers. Bennett is eager to defend Wal-Mart's right to sell the products it chooses, but he doesn't believe that Time Warner should have the same right to sell the rap CDs it chooses or that TV networks should have the right to air the talk shows they want.

Bennett has become our modern-day William Jennings Bryan, a one-time presidential candidate and the lead prosecutor in the Scopes Monkey Trial of 1925. Bryan tried to jail a schoolteacher for teaching evolution because it conflicted with the Bible.

Under brutal cross-examination by defense lawyer Clarence Darrow, Bryan explained that he knew Darwin's theories were wrong because God told him so. Bryan sputtered when Darrow asked if God might have spoken to Charles Darwin, too.

The way it worked, Darrow explained to the court, was that God talked to Bryan, and Bryan told the world. The famous cross-examination, faithfully re-created in the play and movie **Inherit the Wind,** was one of the great victories for truth and freedom in this century, if not an everlasting one.

Mencken, who covered the trial for **The Baltimore Sun**, presciently invoked Bennett when he wrote of Bryan: "What animated him from end to end of his grotesque career was simply ambition—the ambition of a common man to get his hand upon the collar of his superiors, or, failing that, to get his thumb into their eyes. **He was born with a roaring voice, and it had the trick of inflaming half-wits.** His whole career was devoted to raising those half-wits against their betters, that he himself might shine."

Here we are at the end of the 1990s, surrounded by millennial technojabber from our gurus and political leaders, preparing to tramp across that bridge to the twenty-first century, yet we are still slugging out the same question hashed out in Dayton, Tennessee, in July of 1925: Are we free to create, think, and decide for ourselves? Or must we submit to the arrogant notions of those who presume to know what is right for us?

CULTURE WARS

Pat Buchanan is our national Objectivity Poster Boy, a monument to twisted journalistic values. He is the inevitable product of a bankrupt journalistic ideology that permits reporters to speak freely to one another but withhold from readers critical information and impressions that bear directly on our lives.

Voters, viewers, and citizens play a sort of political Russian roulette, hoping that by reading between the lines they can pick up some shred of the truth.

How is it that a politician could be tied to the Aryan Nation, David Duke, and the National Association for the Advancement of White People (the association which provided office space for Buchanan organizers in Louisiana in early 1996)?

How is it that Republicans could stomach a candidate endorsed, as Buchanan was, by the rabid Russian nationalist, Vladimir Zhirinovsky, who instantly recognized a comrade when he saw one? How is it that campaign cochair, the Rev. Donald E. Wildmon, accused by Jewish organizations of reinforcing anti-Semitic stereotypes, could work for Buchanan well into the 1996 primary?

How is it that Buchanan's loyalty to the bigots working for him could be portrayed as another of those quirky but admirable rough-and-tumble character traits of real guys?

I don't ask out of a fondness for rhetorical questions. I ask because I've been thinking about the media coverage of national figures. Specifically, I've been thinking about Nation of Islam leader Louis Farrakhan. Like Buchanan, Farrakhan spews rhetoric that frequently is hateful and inflammatory. Unlike Buchanan, Farrakhan has actually done some good in his life, such as organizing the Million Man March. Farrakhan has actually held a real job, too — running a national spiritual and motivational organization.

Even so, Farrakhan can barely step out in the street without being assaulted by reporters who challenge his commitment to tolerance and remind him of his racially inflammatory statements or bizarre world tours.

Not only does Buchanan get to be a well-paid commentator on national television, he is portrayed as an eloquent and competitive conservative. There he is on the cover of **Time,** wearing a yellow hard hat and gazing up at the sky, the coverline reading: "Grand Old Populists."

How to explain the differences in how the media treat inflammatory public figures like Farrakhan and Buchanan? In a word: racism. Buchanan doesn't come from the world of Black Muslims — a frightening movement for many whites — but from Washington's insider politics and journalism.

Buchanan was not only a commentator on one of Washington's corrupt talk shows, where reporters take money to be "left" or "right" of issues, but he has worked in and around the Washington political structure for years, in both the Nixon and Reagan administrations.

Stuffing your campaign organization with anti-Semites and white supremacists is good ol' hell-raising "populism" — troublesome maybe, but within the rules of the game. Many TV commentators and reporters, especially the

Washington ones, chummily refer to Buchanan as "Pat,"
in a bemused, roll-your-eyes-at-the-rascal way.
Farrakhan only wishes he had it so easy.

O, ORLANDO!

This is a place of totems. You encounter the first one the
minute you step off the plane: Orlando, says the totem, is
a city that takes itself seriously. It means to impress you,
to entertain you, and to do business with you. It has made
up its mind what it wants to be, with a vengeance. It has
embarked on an orgy of totem-building in parallel uni-
verses—the civic and the fantastic.

In an era of tight budgets for local and national government—
in this decade of lowered expectations—Orlando is going
to the moon, thumbing its sunburned nose at the penurious,
exhausted, and dispirited state of most of urban America
in the '90s. Public and civic construction projects have
turned Orlando into one of the world's most popular desti-
nations and bizarre communities on Earth.

Orlando is funding an ambitious project to buy and restore
homes downtown for the urban poor. Orlando has built a
striking new city hall; refurbished a park surrounding a
lake in the heart of town; funded a lavish airport; and con-
structed one of the world's most expensive and impressive
sports arenas to house its beloved basketball team.

Such civic totems are a counterpoint to some strange totems
to technology—the "worlds," theme parks, and "environments" that surround the city. They rise out of the swamps
and run along the highways. The best known are Disney's—
Epcot's Spaceship Earth, Cinderella Castle, the Monorail,
Michael Graves's Dolphin Hotel. But other totems also
surround Orlando—Universal Studios, Sea World, Gator
World, even the Tupperware World Headquarters—and
they reflect the social, cultural, and corporate ethos of the
people who flock here.

To some people, these totems are wasteful follies. To others
they express a community's aspirations. To civic analyst

and author Otis White, America's civic totems—Orlando's spectacles, St. Louis's Gateway Arch, Baltimore's baseball stadium, Chicago's Orchestra Hall, or San Francisco's Golden Gate Bridge—invoke a key question for the community deciding whether to build them: What are we, and what do we want to be?

In Orlando's case, Walt Disney provided the strongest answer to such Lear-like questions. Disney was obsessed in the later years of his life with the construction of the perfect community. **In addition to being a savvy businessman, a mean-spirited boss, and a brilliant designer and producer, Disney was a passionate technological utopian.**
Like other utopians, widely considered the fools of history, Disney believed that technology could be controlled for the common good and that outcomes and communities could be determined by imaginative thinking and careful planning.

Already dying of lung cancer, Disney revealed his dream in 1966 when, for the first time, he publicly referred to "Epcot," his Experimental Prototype Community of Tomorrow.

Epcot, he said, will be "like the city of tomorrow ought to be, a city that caters to the people as a service function. It will be a planned, controlled community, a showcase for American industry and research, schools, cultural and educational opportunities." In Epcot, said Disney, "there will be no slum areas because we won't let them develop. There will be no landowners and therefore no voting control." There will be modest rents, he said, "and no retirees, because everyone will be employed according to their ability. One of our requirements is that the people who live in Epcot must help keep it alive."

Anyone who lives or works in the digital world, or cares what happens to it, should visit Walt Disney's Epcot Center and Tomorrowland. The planners of Tomorrowland and Epcot clearly imagined the millennium to be focused on space and interplanetary travel, and our earthbound lives to be organized around vast open plazas, plenty of sliding doors, metallic voices echoing over unseen loudspeakers, sterile architecture, and Flash Gordon-like citizens wearing buttonless tunics.

But after Disney's death, the corporate-minded elements of his company shelved his plans for a living community and turned Epcot into a vast corporate World's Fair, "presented" by corporations like Exxon, Kodak, AT&T, and United Technologies. Epcot is a business theme park, not a human community.

Ride the escalator to the Tomorrowland Transit Authority and climb aboard the People Mover. The open-air electric train will snake smoothly and slowly above, through, and around Tomorrowland—the strangest and least appealing section of the Magic Kingdom.

Watch, or you'll miss it. Almost one minute into the ride, the People Mover glides into a dark tunnel. "The planners of this community," intones the breathless announcer while the car is still shrouded in inky black, "dared to dream of the perfect community in which to live and work."

Suddenly, fleetingly, on the left, behind a glass enclosure in the darkened tunnel, appears one of the most astonishing sights in Disney World: a breathtaking model of a city. If you are facing forward, you will miss it. The windows and lampposts are lit from within, pinpoint dots of light that outline the model against a darkened backdrop. The model is about ten feet deep and twenty feet long. The effect is eerie: a bold and beautiful city completely out of place in this tunnel above Tomorrowland, as if the idea were to keep it from as many people as possible.

It's a striking vision of a community. Four lean, elegant sky-scrapers of different heights rise above the city center. Broad avenues lead up to them. Several lakes and parks set the buildings off from one another. On the left, an amusement park with a glowing carousel waits in odd contrast, a whimsical touch to keep the town from taking itself too seriously—and a counterpoint, perhaps ironic, to the vast amusement parks of the empire.

Away from the taller buildings are parks, houses, playgrounds,

shops, and apartment buildings spreading out across
the plain. There is plenty of room between buildings, but
the model leaves no doubt that it presumes to be a city.

What is striking about the technologically sophisticated
world Disney inspired is how it mirrors the challenges
facing the emerging digital one. The theme parks are filled
with stunning, jaw-dropping technology—robots, holo-
graphic permeations, 3-D creations, new and interactive
special effects, and digital hat tricks—as is the computer
world. The engineers have done their job of building
gizmos brilliantly, but their visions of technology end when
their projects are done. They can't resist piling one special
effect onto another, even when the result overwhelms
our ability to absorb, enjoy, and use it.

People travel long distances to experience Walt Disney
World, but when they arrive they often can't get on the
rides. With small children they have to stand in the boiling
sun for hours and wait in long lines for food. Exhausted
parents watch the clock, realizing that their time is too
short and their childrens' expectations too high.

At certain times of the day, the crowd density approaches
meltdown—it's almost impossible to move or escape, to
find amusement or comfort. Enchantment and excitement
morph into exhaustion, discomfort, and disappointment.
At night, the music piped out of the ground is often
drowned out by the cries of overstimulated children and
the futile pleas of parents who can't appease them.

We flirt arrogantly, like Disney, with utopian visions. We
often think we're smarter, hipper, different. That our
world will be better, freer, more creative. That it will solve
problems more efficiently and heal the world in new and
more efficient ways. Maybe so.

But we see again and again—from Jules Verne to H. G.
Wells to Disney—that the future is unpredictable. Disney's
tepid, '60s vision of the future was dead wrong. For one
thing, he didn't imagine the Internet. But more importantly,
and more typically, he forgot that new technology has

never staunched the ancient social problems—poverty, crime, violence—that continue to plague us.

NEW YEAR'S NIGHTMARE

New Year's Eve has never been a happy time for me. I don't drink, dance, or look forward to the next day's bowl games. I catch an early movie, curl up in bed with my dogs, read a book, and cackle at all the silly people freezing their butts off in Times Square.

Despite my temperance, I often have nightmares. On the New Year's Eve between 1996 and 1997, I had a dream beyond dreams.

It took place sometime in the future.

It turned out the Cassandras had all been right. **We'd become a nation of screen-addicted zombies.** Several generations of college kids had forsaken beer and sex to sit for hours in front of flickering monitors, just like **The New York Times** warned us about back in '96. Literacy was the name of a hip hop group but had otherwise vanished as a concept. An android engineer in **Star Trek XV** was named Civics, but the word had no other meaning. The Smithsonian's National Museum of American History displayed several violins and batons, an opera ticket stub, and a few books to remind us of our past.

North America had been rearranged geopolitically. The techno elite had clustered in the West, in a prosperous and beautifully landscaped but heavily fortified compound known as the Wired Sector. Their leader was Louis Rossetto. The residents had lots of great stuff and used it freely. They treated one another harshly when they came face-to-face, which happened infrequently, but they were OK if left alone.

Just as predicted during the late '90s cultural-demise hysteria, the East harbored masses of impoverished, angry people with no work and no prospects. And no cool stuff. This domain was ruled by Snoop Doggy Dogg. The people spoke an elaborately profane language and were violent and cruel.

In the Northwest was the fabled Microsoft Nation, led by Bill Gates. Every household had software that turned the bathroom showers on and off, stopped babies from crying, and made adolescents genial.

Every place else was the Wal-Mart Nation, ruled by William Bennett, whose collection of parables was a sacred text. All the culture in this world was blessedly wholesome and uplifting. The TV shows, movies, CDs, and books were about hard-working bumblebees and froggies. And there was a flourishing market in guns and knives.

By and large, the four sectors ignored one another. But one day, **Wired**'s sensors — new and expensive but way-cool technology using massive amounts of RAM — picked up signals showing an alien invasion gathering on the far side of the moon.

The four sector leaders, none of whom were in the habit of speaking to one another, panicked. They agreed to meet.

But there was no public building large enough to accommodate four such egos. Yankee Stadium and the Rose Bowl proved inadequate. So they hit on the only place with room to spare — the new Manhattan Wal-Mart, which ran from Wall Street to Connecticut and sold every "wholesome" consumer product in the world and offered discounts to customers who pledged never to curse or watch violent TV shows.

Surrounded by bodyguards, the four converged on the giant store as thousands of chipper, if clueless, Wal-Mart employees in colorful vests looked on.

Since the four couldn't even agree on the shape of a conference table, each had brought his own means of communication: Rossetto via PC-Web-Meta-TV modem, Dogg by microphone, Bennett via press conference, and Gates through his Microsoft Platform Nerd Projector. If none of the four could speak directly to the others, at least each could hear what the others were saying.

"What are we going to do?" asked Rossetto bluntly. "From my POV, it seems that this is the end of the industrial meta-state as we know it, a meme's end. That's what nobody gets. But how could you? You're all parts of a dying order!"

"Shit," said Snoop Doggy Dogg. "Those motherfuckas put one toe down in my sector, and I'll stick my foot all the way up their asses."

"Now this illustrates the problem," said Bennett angrily. "You're talking filth. Utter garbage. You're a bad example. Have you seen my latest book, Mr. Dogg? It's only $150, and you'll be especially interested in the story, 'The Foul-Mouthed Rapper Who Stopped Talking Dirty, Bought a Suit, and Became Respectable.'"

There was a chuckle from a corner of the vast room. Gates never laughed, but he had a Chuckling program that did it for him. His giant face materialized on the Nerd projector.

"Have some vision," he said. "I foresaw this in 1996, as I told **The New Yorker** then, off the record. We've been working for years on software that will translate Martian into English, auto-operate their spacecraft, and create habitable environments for them here. Talk about Windows, heh-heh. We've already signed $16 billion worth of contracts with the aliens. They won't take one webbed step without using a Microsoft product. Look, I have to get back to my sector now. I'm not used to this much interaction with people, and I have some memos to email everybody. Besides, I've got to oversee the new addition to my 612-acre dining area."

Dogg laughed out loud. "Shit, that's nothing, man. I've already sold the bastards twelve million copies of my new CD, including my hit single, 'Screw U Alien Mothafuckas.'"

Bennett cleared his throat. "You all think you're so smart. In 1997, I created my Alien Empowerment Foundation. And I dashed off a little something called **The Book of Alien Virtues.** The first story is about a Martian who wanted to conquer Earth, so he got up every morning at 4 A.M. for seven million years to build a ship that could travel here. I've got a hundred thousand copies in the warehouse ready to ship. Sort of an uplifting thing. I'm on the **Today Show**

Monday to talk about giving these creatures some values."

Bennett sat back, put his hands behind his head, and guffawed. "Yessir, extraterrestrials need inspiration too. And like I told my agent, there's probably a zillion of 'em."

There was quiet in the room, except for the sound of a keyboard clacking. Rossetto was typing away furiously: "I feel like ROTFLing. This is the reflexive twitching of the postindustrial, premillennial order. None of you gets it." He turned off his laptop.

"OTOH," he said quietly, "do you think these Martians might want to invest in a hot new company with infinite prospects?"

I woke up in a sweat. I went downstairs to be with my family. There was no Snoop Doggy Dogg. No Rossetto. No looming face of Bill Gates.

But William Bennett was on **Good Morning America,** talking about his plan to Empower America.

NET GAIN

"Old media's practice of top-down, father-knows-best journalism is tired, clunky, and obsolete," writes reporter J. D.
Lasica in — of all places — the **American Journalism Review.**
"A more open relationship could be good news for the
future of journalism."

Net culture may be given to heavy-handed cyber rhetoric about
old orders giving way to new ones. Indeed, the notion of
imminent and radical change, of an information revolution
intersecting with the rise of a Digital Age bears truth.

But this doesn't mean that traditional media will or should
expire or that one culture must supplant the other. The
truth is that we need both.

Journalism can survive and prosper in the Digital Age. Citizens
of the often fragmented, diverse, and vast Webbed world
could use the solid facts and reliable reporting of good
journalism. The sensible person will pick what he or she
needs from each.

THINGS NEW MEDIA ARE GOOD AT:

Freedom. New media let people speak far more freely on
politics, sex, religion, and values than old media do. The
online world has no tradition of objectivity — as useless a
journalistic convention as ever existed. Mainstream journalism is not free. It's bounded by the conventions of corporate
owners and timid editors, producers, and publishers.
Interactivity. New media are inherently interactive. Their
capacity for communicating with consumers is limitless.
Community. New media, especially digital media, are by
nature communal; they create new kinds of social clusters
from elderly women to plumbers to black college students.
Fact-driven information and research. The Net makes the
transmission of factual data — not the knee-jerk dogma from
hired-gun spokespeople that's epidemic in old media —

available easily and on demand. On the Net, we can easily assemble not just the liberal or conservative positions, but all sorts of research and opinion almost instantly.

Culture. New media understand that popular culture, from computers to TV to movies, is a precept of American life, not a series of epidemics to be perpetually warned against.

Breaking news. No media relay breaking news and reactions better, more efficiently, or more creatively than digital media.

Transmitting or raising ideas. No medium has ever offered a better means of spreading truth, lies, rumors, or facts than the Web.

Environment for the young. Journalism has relentlessly battled the culture of the young; it has chased them away in droves and now faces the bitter consequence: It has no young readers or viewers. In overwhelming numbers, cable and digital communications are the media of Americans under thirty-five. They are drawn to media that don't find their interests stupid or dangerous.

WHAT TRADITIONAL NEWS OUTLETS DO BETTER:

Present coherent, reliable pictures of the country, the state, the town. By blending text and pictures, and with their inherent portability, newspapers and magazines in particular can give us a picture of the world around us (if only they would). We welcome informed and subjective pieces on race, politics, welfare, and other social issues by writers who gather information, conduct research, and present conclusions.

Compile factual information reliably and accurately. Journalists are trained and experienced fact gatherers. They are far from perfect, but they are the best we have. The good journalists really do want to tell the truth.

Cover the daily workings of government (as opposed to politics). The Web offers tantalizing possibilities, but there are no signs it can present issues and information about government in an accessible, comprehensible, or reliable way— at least not yet.

Publish comics.

Undertake investigative and special reporting. This is an ability nearly limited to mainstream journalism, which has the space, format, and expertise to answer vital political and social questions rather than simply raise them. But most investigative journalism has vanished from daily papers, along with good idiosyncratic writing and varying opinions. **Present major issues and ideas that require detail and sub-stantiation.** Big ideas are better introduced in print than any other medium, a notion relatively few webheads would refute.

THE TECHNOLOGY PART OF THE CULTURE

If there's a bleak note to new media, technology, and politics, it's finding a way for political communities to meet, set agendas, and discuss them in a rational and civil way. Chat rooms on AOL and Pathfinder are often interesting, but so chaotic they're useless as barometers or forums. Flamers, techno-anarchists, the over-testosteroned, the addictively combative, and sometimes the clearly emotionally disturbed still rule the public forums of the digital world, stifling debate, punishing dissent, and forcing serious discussion underground or out of sight. **For all its hype, Web technology is still primitive and unimaginative, permitting mostly random and disjointed discussion or slow and ponderous scrolling through long blocks of text.** The Netizen wrestled all year with hostile postings and disrupted discussions. This may be the Web culture's biggest obstacle.

If public forums aren't made graphically attractive and technologically workable, if they're not moderated or shaped in some rational way, the Web's most cherished philosophy—interactivity—will be discarded as corporations thunder onto the Web. Web media will look increasingly like other media: top-down, elitist, disconnected, and self-righteous. But technology is still certain to change the future of politics. The Net still gives more individuals more voice than any medium in history. The digital world still resonates with a far greater passion for liberty than its offline journalistic cousins have shown for two hundred years.

The Internet is putting in place the machinery to transmit facts, opinion, and argument to more people more quickly than ever.

DIGITAL PHOENIX

Critics, pundits, academics, and scholars are lining up to declare the end of one thing or another. A major newspaper recently reported the end of fashion. A book appearing in early 1996 described a nearly terminal malaise afflicting democracy.

Professors are filling academic journals with articles heralding the end of journalism. Critic Arthur Danto writes of the end of art. Science writer John Horgan has released a new book called **The End of Science: Facing the Limits of Knowledge in the Twilight of the Scientific Age** (Helix, 1996). Rochelle Gurstein, a writer and teacher in New York, wrote a book called **The Repeal of Reticence: Cultural and Legal Struggles over Free Speech, Obscenity, Sexual Liberation, and Modern Art** (Hill & Wang, 1996).

The big idea in politics seems to be the end of big government (and tax cuts), and the big idea in culture is that civilization and morality as we know them are winding down.

This termination of human creativity and discovery seems to be somehow connected to the approach of the new millennium, as if we're already busy marking the end of one era to prepare for the next one.

In the digital world, the atmosphere could hardly be more different. All that mourning, pronouncing, lamenting, and closure seem to netizens to chronicle a dispirited and pessimistic society. On the Net, there is not the sense of an era ending, but of a remarkable one beginning: the start of the Digital Age—a millennial idea if ever there was one.

The clacking of keyboards might as well be hammers pounding on nails. Online, a new culture is emerging day by day.

The Jesus Homepage is gently poking fun at sacred dogma. Bubbe's Back Porch in Cyborganic Gardens is redefining biography.

The Well is ponderously arguing about media and thrashing out the future of telecommunications. **Salon** is adding literacy and no small measure of civility to the Web. America Online is redefining the possibilities of online chat. **Slate** has charitably given insider Washington journalists who went to Harvard a place to publish online. The Netizen is struggling to reconcile attitude with civic responsibility. Microsoft is tossing up Cityscape Web sites that encourage us to dine out and to explore new kinds of urban-based digital communities.

Suck is brashly in place, eager to deflate the cyberpompous wherever they appear. **Bitch** is empowering digital women; on SeniorNet, the elderly have ended years of isolation by forming one of the world's most striking and supportive communities. NetNoir is drawing middle-class African Americans online. Cypherpunks are wreaking anarchic havoc. And in the lawless corners of cyberspace, hackers are launching mailbombs from obscure Usenet groups.

All across the online world, the young are patching together their own culture, writing software, and spinning out homepages—to the sometimes derisive, fearful, or contemptuous hoots of their elders.

Each day, the digital culture continues to emerge as one of the world's most vigorous, fascinating, and ascendant—in dramatic contrast to an entrenched culture rushing to pronounce itself DOA and well past resuscitation.

THE INTERACTIVE COLUMNIST (REDUX)

WOMEN IN SKIVVIES

The Olympic Games in 1996 were a horror show for women—a major setback in getting media to portray them as more than vulnerable, overly emotional, cute, devious, and sexual creatures.

NBC abandoned all sensitive portrayals of women to boost ratings and make money. It accomplished both with stunning success. NBC reminded every publisher, producer, and editor in America that stereotypes still have a huge appeal and are often good for business. The cost to women, however, will be dear.

Of course, many women have reveled in the vapid characters their sisters play in movies and romance novels, breathless prime-time docudramas, soap operas, and talk shows.

Nevertheless, recent movies have managed to include female heroes, and women more and more frequently pop up on TV as successful, capable individuals, with families and careers—or living well on their own. Some of the most blatant sexist media stereotypes have been beaten back.

But this progress suffered an enormous setback at the hands of NBC. The network's blatant emotional manipulation of female athletes and viewers could not have been missed by a single one of the widget makers who run America's big media—and now have an even better idea of the profits to be made through pandering to stereotypes.

NBC should have called its portrayal of female athletics "Women in Skivvies." **Most of the women we got to see perform were wearing bathing suits or leotards.**

Some of the most dramatic athletic contests involving women—basketball, soccer, and softball—received only cursory coverage. Usually, NBC didn't even assign correspondents. We were shown these athletes mostly in medal ceremonies, where there was at least some chance they might cry while the cameras zoomed hopefully toward their corneas.

Female swimmers, runners, and cyclists were constantly rumored to be embroiled in catfights or gossip sessions—NBC created an entirely new, internationally broadcast cultural stereotype—the female celebrity athlete as Superbitch.

But the most disturbing portraits were of the painfully perky gymnasts. What different expectations we hold for male and female athletes! How frequently journalism exploits this sickening trend rather than exposing it.

While male gymnasts whizzed over and around bars and rings, the athlete-children of "women's" gymnastics (years younger than their male counterparts) sobbed bitterly after disappointments and defeats. Then they were cuddled by male coaches who thought nothing of risking their injury for the greater glory of TV.

The entire scenario recalled some Dickensian nightmare in which helpless children are orphaned and abandoned to the mercy of greedy men. The emblem of **this** Olympic Games—an injured Kerri Strug crawling in agony off the mat—was offered as a poignant picture, a story to elicit admiration. What it should have provoked was not admiration, but outrage that an injured young woman was imperiled to win a medal for the team.

These girls' lives seem to have been manipulated right out from under their bandaged feet.

BACKLASH

I received several hundred email messages about my view of NBC's portrayal of Olympic women and its blatant efforts to appeal to female viewers by obsessing on the personal travails of female athletes and their internecine conflicts.

About 60 percent of the messages were from men, who disagreed that women were portrayed in sexist ways. They pointed out that Kerri Strug is over eighteen years old and free to make her own choices about whether she wants to risk injury.

Most of the messages from men were intelligent, thoughtful, and convincing. They left me feeling, in fact, that my rant was too strident. I remain convinced that much of NBC's profiling of women was treacly and overly personal, but I took note.

Women who sent email, on the other hand, overwhelmingly agreed that the coverage of female athletes was patronizing and overly emotional. And they agreed: NBC gave too little air time to increasingly popular women's sports such as basketball, soccer, and softball. They also echoed my sentiment that the ceaseless narratives of athletes overcoming obstacles en route to Atlanta were tiresome and false.

Many of the women who wrote me, however, felt that NBC broadcast more positive images of female athletes than my column gave it credit for.

I stand corrected.

MY TAKE ON TUPAC

Sometime deep in the coming millennium, long after the culture wars now raging in America have fizzled, the rapper Tupac Shakur will be remembered as one of the seminal figures in the evolution of American popular culture.

Shakur embodied Shakespeare's notion of tragedy—he was gifted, charismatic, violent, and self-destructive. He was shot to death in Las Vegas September 7, 1996, at the age of twenty-five. Known mostly for his irate rap lyrics and his imprisonment for sexual assault, Shakur's work is one snapshot in the increasingly nasty battles over the explicitness of popular culture.

The battles have been long-brewing. As violence, drug epidemics, and economic problems among innercity youths worsened during the '80s—when the bullet became the leading cause of death for young American black men— rap, especially gangsta rap, became angrier and more provocative.

You could look at rap in two ways—the cause of societal decay or the symptom. For the most part, journalists and politicians chose the former, since they didn't know what to do or say about the latter. Shakur, Snoop Doggy Dogg, Ice-T, and other rappers became the most controversial, reviled figures on the entertainment landscape—and easy targets for demagogues like William Bennett, politicians like Dan Quayle, and celebrity blockheads like Charlton Heston.

Meanwhile, the idea that music causes violence has become mainstream. The notion that culture is dangerous has even been embraced by some feminists, boomers, and Democrats—including Bill Clinton and Al Gore.

Shakur was one of the cultural conservatives' pet examples of how rap degrades the young, promotes violence—is as dangerous as it is vulgar. In 1992, a Texas state trooper was killed by a teenager who was reportedly listening to Shakur's **2Pacalypse Now,** which included songs about killing police officers.

Then-vice president Dan Quayle, one of a long line of politicians to exploit popular culture as a political issue, demanded the album be barred from release.

Interscope, Shakur's record label, refused, but the flap spotlighted angry rappers and helped Bennett lead his eventually successful campaign to force Time Warner to drop its investment in Interscope. Later, it was determined that the killer didn't own the tape in question.

Of course, today Interscope is selling CDs like crazy, many of them Shakur's. His 1995 album **Me Against the World** (Out Da Gutta/Interscope) burst onto the Billboard chart at Number One and sold two million copies. After Shakur's release from prison in October 1995, he began recording **All Eyez on Me** (Death Row/Interscope), which has sold millions of copies.

Shakur was an outlaw artist who worked and lived outside the approval and respectability awarded by the media, much of the African-American political community, and the corporate entertainment world. He was assaulted by pack journalists and powerful politicians. He was supported only by his many fans—black and white.

The more reviled he was, the more popular Shakur became. Our many moral guardians saw this as a confirmation of moral decay. **In fact, Shakur's rise signifies the largely unnoticed mass rebellion of the young, who are taking advantage of the first era in history when they have the means and machinery to make their own cultural choices.**

It will be a long time before we can rate the artistic merit of rap, or weigh it against other musical forms equally reviled in their time. But Tupac Shakur will prove as historic a figure in the annals of modern media as Dan Rather, Barbara Walters, or Walter Cronkite.

TUPACKLASH

The Media Rant Code of Ethics stipulates that when response to a column is universally, eloquently, and sweepingly critical, the author is obliged to share this with his or her readers.

Tupac Shakur's significance, in my mind, was not his character—or lack thereof—but that he couldn't have existed in the American pop culture pantheon a generation ago.

I knew I'd struck some nerves when the very first email response read, "I usually like your column, but you can take this one and stick it up your lily-livered white ass."

No wonder so many journalists fear interactivity. This is nothing like the days when I wrote columns for **New York** and **Rolling Stone**: I was free to take any position I wanted, and absolutely nobody could—or did—reach me for days, or weeks, on end.

A year of intense Web writing has taught me, among other things, that a column generally elicits one of five types of response:

1. A balanced but subdued response from readers: Some people agree, some people don't, but nobody gets tied up in knots.

2. A great outpouring of praise and support: This does happen, but it is distressingly rare.
3. A miraculous debate: Only slightly less rare than response 2, these dialogues (among my readers, but also including me) sometimes go on for weeks, even months, and greatly enhance understanding about the subject.
4. A fevered response from advocates and ideologues: anti-abortion adherents, NRA supporters, anyone from the Christian Right, liberals scouring the Web for signs of insensitivity, conservatives whining that their point of view is never represented—the list goes on and on.
5. Near-unanimous hoots, jeers, and insults: the rarest response and the most intriguing.

When the hoots and jeers become deafening, something's wrong. Either the premise of the column is faulty or I failed to express myself clearly. It's also possible, of course, that I'm taking a courageous stand in the face of overwhelming opposition. Right?

The Shakur column touched off unprecedented jeers: "This guy was just a scum," an African-American accountant wrote of Shakur. "I just can't mourn him or elevate him to historical importance as you're foolishly doing."

An academic wrote: "Is this just knee-jerk PC stuff? If so, it's atypical, and shame on you!"

"Look," wrote an attorney, "the fact that the media reported that Shakur was a misogynistic thug doesn't mean he wasn't. The point you're missing is that a lot of these rappers are responsible for a lot of violence against women and for a cheap attitude that hurts minority kids. Rappers like Shakur reinforce the worst instincts of many underclass kids. For that, he deserved to be shot and good riddance to him."

Not a single emailer said he or she liked the column or offered a good word about Shakur. The silence stands in poignant contrast to the millions of CDs he sold to mostly young kids. Were they all gullible misogynists?

Violent, dope-fiend, girlfriend-beating white rock stars are never expected to be positive role models for white America. Blaming rap for underclass violence is an easy way to avoid the difficult and more explosive issues facing the urban poor and, increasingly, the suburban and rural poor: that children are having children, that people are stuck in bad jobs, that familial chaos reigns, that schools SUCK, that drugs and guns are everywhere.

I **could** argue that the best rappers have seized the role that journalists have been shirking: raising hell about the mayhem and misery among the nation's underclass.

But I'd rather offer an honest explanation. My soft spot for Shakur stems not only from the belief that he was a talented and vivid writer who seemed, by some accounts, to be finally settling down, but that he and fellow rappers have been largely abandoned to wage solo battle with moral guardians, censors, and demagogues—while liberals, reporters, libertarians, webheads, and others scream in outrage every time their own freedoms are besieged.

Shakur was a messed-up man who sprang from an angry culture awash in poverty and blood and somehow created powerful messages about his life. That makes him more than just another street thug to me.

TUPACKLASH, TAKE TWO

On the Web, if nobody's pissed at you, that means you're dead. Evidently, I'm alive and well.

The Tupac Shakur flap lasted for days. Although the reaction was initially critical, it soon after turned supportive. Now it is morphing into a terrific email yak-a-thon involving music producers, teachers, moral guardians, a couple of Shakur's high school classmates, concerned boomer mommies and daddies, enraged African-American Baptists, black and white college kids, and increasingly stuffy webheads clucking away about violent imagery.

Sucksters have been rabidly critical of my columns. Cypherpunks have been hounding me everywhere. **My boss has**

**joined Threads, calling me a TV-phobe and suggesting I am
white, bald, and fat.**

Web pile-ons are irresistible to flamers—those anarchic
cypherpunks who are drawn to the scent of blood—and
this one was a classic of the genre. I felt sorry for myself
for a bit, then decided that if my job was to spark discussion, I was doing OK. I had sparked a month's worth
in a week.

I should point out that the harshest critics post publicly
in Threads while supporters generally send me private
email. Threads are for disagreements: Webheads don't do
much public praising.

But I should also make it clear that in nearly a year
of writing on and about the Web, I've come to intensely
dislike bullies who assault people while hiding behind
false names and drive out the newcomers and the timid.
And I also can't help wondering at the well-meaning but
apparently witless people who give them the chance to
do this in the name of free speech.

It's important that the bullies never win.

I've learned to separate the bullies—at once clever and
cowardly—from my many thoughtful critics and to value
criticism more than I ever had thought imaginable when I
wrote in a different medium. I know much more about
music, rap, culture, and kids than I knew last week—tons
more. When I write about it again, I'll do a better job of it.

Hail interactivity. It works.

THE WEB MEETS WAL-MART

Are you serious about protecting free speech? Do you want
to choose your own music? Do you respect the creative
freedom of artists and their right to profit from their work?
Do you fear the devastating impact America's megacorporations can have on creative freedom and choice?
Then boycott Wal-Mart stores.

And urge everyone you know to do the same.

The single largest seller of pop music in America—to the tune of fifty-two million CDs last year—Wal-Mart is forcing songs to be removed, cover designs to be changed, and lyrics that its executives find offensive to be altered. It's bullying studios to make tamer and safer films as well. Since Wal-Mart refuses to carry any CDs with a "parental advisory" notice, artists and record labels say they're under increasing pressure to sanitize their work. Those who disagree with the Wal-Mart notions of morality are deprived of revenue.

One example: The chain's stores, according to **The New York Times,** refused to carry Sheryl Crow's new album because of a lyric about Wal-Mart selling guns to children. When Crow refused to excise the lines, she lost 10 percent of her album's potential sales.

Wal-Mart won't sell CDs with explicit rap lyrics or with sexual references. (Of course, it's happy to carry rifles, knives, handcuffs, and handgun ammunition.)

The threat to the freedom of ideas and artistic expression by companies like Wal-Mart is far greater than threats posed by, say, the essentially toothless and unenforceable Communication Decency Act, which so exercised netizens in '95 and '96.

Wal-Mart stores dominate rural and suburban communities. Kids in these areas are at the mercy of Wal-Mart's dictating what wholesome culture is, especially since the chain is driving out smaller music outlets that actually care about music and know something about it.

Unlike chains that have moved aggressively into the book business but are experienced book retailers with little interest in censoring books (like Borders and Barnes & Noble), Wal-Mart is a discount retailer with **no** expertise in music and **no** respect for individual choice or creativity.

No entities are more dangerous to popular culture than powerful corporations with political agendas. They suck up all the space around them and force the makers of creative products to submit. As these companies evolve toward commercializing the Internet, their noxious censoring will much more seriously threaten the freedom of information than the CDA ever might have.

Net culture is the best available weapon to combat this arrogant expansion of power by a corporation that presumes to know what moral and artistic choices its customers—and, indirectly, the rest of us—should be allowed to make.

We can take on Wal-Mart and other corporations that are growing obscenely powerful and threaten the freedom of commerce and freedom of ideas.

The Net is the best means of disseminating the message that Wal-Mart's entertainment retailing policies are unacceptable. Spread the word:

- Wal-Mart stores should be boycotted until the company agrees to respect the free movement of ideas and the right of consumers—even young ones—to make their own choices about values.
- Wal-Mart, if it insists on mucking with music, should label altered products clearly.

Music and movie lovers, liberals and libertarians: Get together and picket Wal-Mart stores. Tell parents that the company is making familial decisions for them and their children, mislabeling the products it sells, and taking upon itself the cultural policing of the country.

Record companies, show some spunk: Sell uncensored CDs on the Web. Defend your artists **and** make money via the miracle of digital sales. Give your consumers the option to buy original, uncensored versions.

Voters: Mailbomb, snailbomb, and telephone-torture your legislators. Urge your Congress member to support legislation that would force Wal-Mart to clearly label CDs and videos that have been altered, often without the permission or knowledge of the artist.

Readers: Email Wal-Mart's president and tell him what you think.

Websters: Give isolated teenagers the original lyrics of songs, especially of those banned by Wal-Mart because

the company's purchasers don't like them. The Web culture
should become the first medium to support kids' rights
to control more of their own decisions. And don't stop at
the Web! Compile mailing lists! Post to newsgroups!
Since when are the likes of Sam Walton allowed to set the
country's artistic agenda?

CULTURE CLASH

What a shock it was that my column on Wal-Mart generated
far more email than any other column in 1996. Even more
shocking, virtually all of the respondents were critical,
disapproving, or outraged by what I wrote.
Anybody who doubts that art, family, and morality are a red-
hot political issue should take on this one.
With a handful of exceptions, the email was overwhelmingly
critical of my assertion that Wal-Mart should be boycotted.
Concern ran higher for Wal-Mart's freedom to stock whatever merchandise it wants, in whatever form it wants, than
for the rights of singers, artists, or producers to make the
music and movies they want.

"What about the right of a store to decide what merchandise it will carry?" messaged Ben. "While you may not
agree with their policies, they are far from censorship."
"You ought to have your head examined," Larry wrote.
"As a police officer, my job is hard enough as it is without
gangster rap groups telling youths to kill cops."
And from mtl: **"Why don't you and your boycotters 'goose-step'
in gestapo type fashion to boycott freedom? The freedom NOT
to sell slime and garbage....** How 'bout that, Mr. Marxist!"
Emailers praised Wal-Mart's low prices and expressed appreci-
ation that the company had taken a stand against what it
perceives to be immoral.
Ironically, some of the few supportive posters were not the
Web's famed libertarians, but gun-rights advocates, who
felt Wal-Mart should not be pressuring artists to alter their
work any more than the store should be withdrawing guns

and ammunition from its shelves.

They were, however, critical of my juxtaposing Wal-Mart's refusal to sell uncensored music with its willingness to sell guns. On this score, they were right: The issues are not linked.

It became clear that many of the emails — several containing identical letters of support for Wal-Mart — reflected an organized effort. I suspect they were dispatched from religious groups unhappy with the state of popular culture. Many of the messages that accused me of trying to censor Wal-Mart had virtually identical language.

Perhaps that contributed to the unprecedented volume, which had exceeded two thousand within a week.

There was, however, one email that made the whole exercise worthwhile: "I am glad," wrote Rusty from Utah, "that people like you are standing up for people like me (I'm 15 years old) who have no voice in the world because people think that we are stupid."

To the up-in-arms, the deeply religious, the gun collectors, and those who wrote to me defending conservative and religious values, our common ground is this: We should be free to make our own choices. Wal-Mart isn't permitting us to do that. It's making them for us before products can get to us. And cashing in on this hypocrisy and fake piety as well. Wal-Mart is censorious, greedy, hypocritical, and deceptive.

Wal-Mart is a powerful example of the impact of economic censorship, which is often far more devastating to creativity and free speech than other kinds of abridgement. Many webheads view censorship as evil only if it comes from government. But corporations can censor information and culture much more pervasively than government, and it is just as troubling when they do.

Wal-Mart is forcing changes in music and movies that government wouldn't dare attempt — it would be slammed with outrage and fury if it tried. In its campaign to clean up America, Wal-Mart goes beyond simply refusing to carry CDs it finds offensive. It carries the work of artists otherwise deemed offensive only if the jackets are changed and the lyrics are altered or deleted by the record companies.

For an enormous stretch of this country, Wal-Mart is the only music retailer for miles around. It's famous for driving off smaller stores and competing chains. Wal-Mart's actions don't signify freedom. They deprive people of freedom of choice. The chain then profits from the very same artists whose original work it deems offensive. Wal-Mart deceives its customers—it lets them buy creative content that has been altered without telling them.

The retailer is changing the way movies and music are made in America. Does it have the right? Sure, if it can get away with it.

Do we have the right to shop elsewhere? You bet.

Please do.

WAL-MART AND ME: A WHIRLWIND TOUR

Two days after my first Wal-Mart column, my computer crashed under a mailbomb campaign from Wal-Mart supporters. This assault, which included mailbomb duplicating programs, viruses, and old-fashioned hate mail, went on for four days.

I've never struck such a nerve with my column.

Want a whirlwind tour of my education?

Typically, the older the emailers were, and the more rural, the more supportive they were of efforts to turn the cultural clock back to a saner, more "moral" time. They saw Wal-Mart as an entity finally willing to take a stand against the corrosive garbage pouring into their communities online, via music, and through TV. They fear rap—and blame it for crime, illegitimate births, and, more generally, the decline of America.

The digerati, the information elites, who live mostly in urban centers like New York, San Francisco, Austin, or Chicago, take their liberal access to culture pretty much for granted. Skilled computer users, they are used to accessing what ever they want via the Web, if not at retail stores. They have little firsthand experience of censorship.

Many digerati found it ludicrous that anybody would buy CDs at Wal-Mart at all. They were even more startled to learn—many just refused to believe it—that Wal-Mart is the largest pop music retailer in America. They were skeptical that a discount retail chain could possibly have much influence on culture, music, or movies.

By far the most powerful email I received was from young people in more remote places—Utah, parts of the South, the Midwest. Their anger and frustration at being dependent on stores like Wal-Mart was striking. Many told of seeing Wal-Mart arrive in their communities; they watched as their favorite music, clothing, and retail stores—where they could buy things that helped them express their individuality—vanished. These are kids who have no choice but to buy sanitized CDs or, in the case of many rap artists, not buy them at all.

Many recounted buying a Wal-Mart CD only to go home and hear blank spots, interrupted songs, or songs completely missing. Many talked of angry and fearful parents who would destroy on sight CDs they didn't like, rifle through their mail for contraband music, search their rooms for CDs with unwholesome lyrics or titles, forbid time online.

For these kids, the loss of music stores, havens, and gathering spots for fans and compadres was profound. For them, seeing favorite artists and TV shows and getting online were constant struggles. **They are powerfully fighting the Wal-Marting of their lives.**

Despite the fact that this entire controversy was about them, their culture, and their futures, most of the email I received talked over and around them, as if they didn't really exist as human beings capable of making moral or rational choices.

Hostility toward juveniles is palpable. Most partisans of Wal-Mart are either indifferent to what younger people think or simply see them as too vulnerable and weak-minded to participate in discussions about themselves.

My mail showed that the libertarian streak on the Web is profound. Initially, there was great support for the right of Wal-Mart or other corporations to buy and sell what they wanted. As the week wore on, however, many of the libertarians perceived that Wal-Mart was going further than simply making sales choices. Few would fault Borders for failing to stock pornographic books, for example.

Many offered to write Wal-Mart and urge the company to moderate its cultural crusade — in their letters they would express their support for the idea that nobody should tell a company what or what not to sell.

Was there a common ground in these messages? I thought so. In different ways and from vastly different perspectives, these people almost all ended up saying the same thing: Freedom is important. They're willing to take the trouble to fire off messages about it — and keep on talking about these issues even when there is enormous disagreement.

The digital community is often criticized for creating narcissistic enclaves in which the like-minded talk to the like-minded. Not true. My column moved through many strata of society, from college students to Wal-Mart employees to parents crusading for "decency" to teenage Web sites and mailing lists. I heard from cops, priests, small retailers, music industry executives, rabid evangelicals, outspoken libertarians, and rural gun owners. Proof that the Web is a hive that sends ideas whizzing through different levels of politics and society was borne out here.

There is great potential in this kind of communication. Probably not many minds were changed, but there was a softening of positions. I had the sense that if this discussion were continued, we could find a position most of the people writing me would be comfortable with.

My unexpectedly intense freedom tour through the Web got a lot of people with radically different points of view talking to me — then, more importantly, to one another.

It would be silly to romanticize or exaggerate the impact of the dialogue or its outcome. But it was a new kind of political conversation.

It was no longer a private dialogue between Wal-Mart and the record companies. It was not a dialogue dominated by pundits, talk-show hosts, priests, or politicians.

It was a conversation very much in the open, for and about us. It is, after all, our culture, our money, and our choice.

CODA

Martha L., a 67-year-old church elder from Tennessee, messaged me one weekend.

"I'm sure you're a nice young man," she said. "But this boycott talk is very negative. Can't you set a better example to young people and think of something positive?"

Martha had told me earlier that week that I was an unwitting but dangerous tool of Satan. She sent me a letter she had sent to Wal-Mart, in which she prayed for the store to hold the line against popular music, which she called a "virus," and other forms of degenerate filth emanating from TV and movies.

She may have had a point about the devil, and she **definitely** had one about the boycott talk. (There's something retro about a boycotting — it conjures up the fuzzy-headed politics of the '60s.)

Martha got me wondering if there wasn't a more enlightened, maybe high-tech approach to this little cultural brawl we're having on The Netizen. Maybe some way to propel the issue across that bridge to the twenty-first century.

Miraculously, a reader with the handle Lostchild emailed me right after Martha.

"This Web music store, Tunes, could be a great alternative to the Wal-Marts of the world," he wrote. "They promise to stock a variety of styles and have a plan for community building around common tastes. They deserve credit for having the right idea."

We should have thought of this earlier. **Boycott Wal-Mart by all means, but even smarter — shop the Web.**

Tunes is among a growing number of Web music outlets that deserve lots of credit and definitely have the right idea. Amazon.com books is making lots of money selling books on the Web. So why not music sites that offset corporate efforts to censor culture? It's the perfect interactive offense—a great digital mooning—to the Wall of Decency that Wal-Mart is trying to build around our music and popular culture.

For an example of how the Web offers consumer freedom, check out Tunes. Through the emerging technology called intelligent agents, visitors can browse 200,000 song previews and rate what they hear. Tunes will then offer suggestions as to what customers might like. They can also search through the Tunes database, which Tunes says contains a million song titles, 200,000 albums, and 163,000 artists. Shoppers can buy CDs and tapes—Tunes has more than 150,000 titles. Members (membership is optional) can send and receive TunesMail and build individual music profiles and creative play lists. You need Real Audio 3.0 and a 28.8 modem to hear the songs but not to browse or shop.

Tunes joins Firefly, CDNow, CDworld, and other online music outlets that are giving anyone with a computer and modem a music selection that's beyond the wildest dreams of any kid in a Wal-Mart-dominated middle-American town.

Tunes and Firefly offer a preview of interactive shopping. Like Wal-Mart, the sites want to make money. But in the spirit of interactive culture, both give users the tools to create a musical community shaped by the interests and tastes of shoppers, rather than simply a vehicle by which morality is arbitrarily forced down the throats of consumers through abuse of arrogant and predatory corporate power.

Unlike Wal-Mart, Tunes wants to serve everybody. It sells Christian and gospel music and other wholesome stuff.

In fact, through Tunes I purchased Walter Howard's **Whatever You Want, God's Got It.** This was my Christmas gift for Martha. Her first contact with me, remember, consisted of calling me an agent of the devil. I would, she warned, burn in hell. I hope she likes her tunes. I bought it after she wrote this to me late in the fall: "This is quite a dustup. I'm going to send you some cookies."

Martha was as good as her word: two days before Christmas, a metal bin of raisin cookies arrived, wrapped neatly in brown paper and carefully tied.

In it was a handwritten note on the back of a plain white card. "Mr. Katz," she said. "I told the women on my committee that I was writing this to you and sending my cookies — they're a big item around here! Everyone was very curious about it. Some people thought it was odd, to say the least."

"I hope you and your family enjoy them, though. I expect we will never meet, though if you come this way, I hope you'll drop by. At my age, invitations aren't casual. I've enjoyed our notes back and forth, although I never even heard of a computer just a few years ago and sometimes shake my head at my own gall. I think I'm right and you're wrong much of the time, but we don't need to get into that at Christmastime, do we? Have a lovely holiday and a happy New Year. We can start arguing again in January."

AFTERWORD

A writer who relishes challenges and criticisms from readers can hardly expect an afterword to his book that merely seconds his opinions. Or so I hope. Jon Katz's media rants are provocative, energized, and energizing—but his enthusiasm for the digital culture is not always contagious. So I thank him for opening a lively, timely conversation, and, secure in the belief that he expects only to "get the first word, but never the last," I offer these misgivings.

The benefit of this emerging culture—interactivity, speed of communication, spontaneity of discussion, access to information, and opportunities to disseminate it widely— all have their costs. Interactivity can easily devolve into hyperactivity; spontaneity of expression can be the enemy of thoughtfulness; the power of every individual or group to disseminate facts is also the power to disseminate rumors. That the UN is going to invade the US, that weird weather reflects an increase in alien invasions, that gay people regularly engage in bestiality are only a few of the "facts" you can pick up in cyberspace. You don't have to be an elitist mediaphobe to find the rantings of many netizens no less mindless, and a bit more hostile, than the chatter of newscasters striving to make us like them.

Interactivity has the virtue of democracy, conferring upon everyone the right and opportunity to be heard, but it is also saddled with democracy's vice—a tendency to assume that everyone who has a right to be heard has something to say that's worth hearing. It is a common misconception that plagues the most traditional public forums: people stand up at town meetings and demand that their neighbors respect their opinions, not simply the right to utter them.

It is one of the ironies of democracy that this confusion often turns out to be more subversive than supportive of public **respect** for free speech. When you begin by equating defense of the **right** to speak with defense of the **particular**

speech at issue, you end by conditioning the right to speak on the defense of what's said. You take on the easy fight for freedom of the speech you like, decamping from the struggle to protect the speech you hate.

I'm not suggesting that interactivity will foster intolerance of free speech among netizens. The unusually high value they place on untrammeled free expression, for its own sake, should overcome the impulse to censor. But while interactivity and the commitment to raucous debate are invigorating, they are also apt to produce cacophony and a preference for speaking over thinking.

The Net is not a quiet place, conducive to contemplation. It is easy to say that we can retreat from it as we need, that the new digital culture can coexist with a traditional literary one, but I suspect that the taste for quiet and solitude will be bred out of people for whom expression is by nature interactive. Writing and reading in cyberspace are, as Katz so clearly describes, different from the writing and reading we used to know, to which some of us cling.

For me, writing, like thinking, is an independent, introspective activity, not a collaborative one; it requires quiet solitude. I experience every one of my essays and every book as a conversation with myself. I write partly to discover what I think. Of course I want to engage readers and provoke debate among them, but, while I'm writing, the thoughts of my prospective readers are rarely as interesting to me as my own.

You can accuse me of being self-absorbed, but with some exceptions, like pure reportage, writing begins with self-absorption, as every diarist, perhaps most fiction writers, and many columnists can attest. Some of my readers may well be smarter, more informed, or blessed with better judgment than I. Still I learn more from doing my work than from heeding reactions to it. In fact, I purposefully avoid showing anyone an article or book until it's completed: I don't want to be influenced by criticism or praise. I don't want to be distracted.

This doesn't mean that I write without knowing what other people have written or thought about my subject.

It doesn't mean that I'm cloistered and bereft of interactions. For me, serious writing is always preceded by reading and often includes some historical study. I am not only engaged in a conversation with myself; I'm continuing a public conversation, which, in various guises, predates and may outlive me. I'm contributing one particular point of view, with no hope or desire for resolution. I want my views to be informed, but I don't shape them by a process of consensus. And often my readers do not know more than I do about my subject, because they haven't had the luxury of studying and thinking about it for months, or years.

So, when Jon Katz says the Web taught him that he is never "completely right," that he is "merely a transmitter of ideas waiting to be improved by people who know more," I say that he was unduly confident before he began inhabiting the Web and is unduly modest now. No one is ever completely right, and no writer worth publishing is a mere apprentice to his readers.

We read partly to learn; we seek out writers who seem to know more than we do or have thought longer about matters that interest us. The impatience with many pundits and journalists that Katz expresses and many people feel reflects the irritating fact that they **don't** seem to know more than the rest of us; they just talk more. Their authority is unearned. It's not superior knowledge that makes them seem arrogant but lack of it.

But journalists are not monolithic. Many of us can probably name at least a few we consider worth heeding. We come to trust particular writers and even pundits because we come to know them a little; at least we become familiar with their voices and viewpoints—just as we become familiar with particular magazines, newspapers, and networks. That knowledge provides us with context for the opinions and information we receive—essential context often missing on the Net.

In cyberspace, we converse with strangers who may or may not reveal their identities and agendas. We can't even know the sex of our conversants, much less their biases, the sources of their facts or opinions, or the validity of their claims to expertise. Because we don't know the provenance of so much information circulating throughout the digital culture, we cannot evaluate its credibility. How, then, do we distinguish rumor from fact?

Katz is alert to the problems attendant on anonymity, notably verbal abuse, but I am more concerned with misinformation than incivility. What's worrisome about anonymity is not just its intimidation of the thin-skinned but its seduction of the gullible. Skepticism would arm people against rumormongering, and Katz might assure us that netizens are, indeed, rather skeptical. But, he points out, they are primarily mistrustful of government and the mainstream media; they assume that politicians and journalists lie. That's not skepticism; it's nihilism (some politicians and journalists do tell the truth, at least some of the time), and nihilism engenders gullibility, as Hannah Arendt observed. Arendt attributed the power of modern propaganda partly to a popular tendency to believe "everything and nothing," to think that "everything [is] possible and that nothing [is] true." People who automatically disbelieve politicians and journalists may instead believe in angels and UFOs. For those who reflexively assume that government officials always lie, official denials of a report that TWA flight 800 was shot down by friendly fire become confirmation of its truth. Sometimes the digital culture seems like one in which Oliver Stone sets the standard for investigative journalism.

Whether or not the New Rationalism promised by the Net prevails over the New Irrationalism, inhabiting cyberspace will probably change the way we reason, as well as the way we read. Hypertext will be the death of arguments — those tightly structured skeins of logic that require readers to be attentive, undistracted by linkages. And, people who learn how to write on computers learn to devalue coherency, one of the virtues of linear thinking. This is how the typical writing guide today teaches students to write essays: Conceive five main points. Construct a paragraph around each, then arrange and rearrange the paragraphs until you're satisfied by their order. What's lost is the notion of an essay as an integral, organic creation that develops naturally from conception to conclusion, not merely a collection of interchangeable paragraphs or parts. Do I sound like a curmudgeon, resistant to change? Perhaps. Surely old processes of thinking will be replaced by new ones with values all their own. Surely we're not getting stupider; we're simply getting smart in different ways. But the benefits of our developmental leaps will be limited by the abruptness of change and consequent disconnections between the old culture and the new. "Like the [American] colonists, the Net community has a distinct sense of itself as a separate political entity," Katz writes. I hope he's wrong about this, because I think he's right when he stresses the importance of extending access to this community to reduce the gulf between the "technologically equipped and the technologically deprived." I'm not encouraged by his view of the typical netizen as a politically disengaged libertarian hostile to social welfare programs.

Katz offers a welcome critique of culturephobes, like William Bennett, who blame cultural trends for economic and social ills. People obsess about the speculative effects of violent images on children, he observes, and ignore the indisputable effects of poverty. Netizens no doubt join in this attack on Bennett and other defenses of decency, but, if Katz's assessment is accurate, they're unconcerned with the neglect of social welfare. Indeed, the digital culture that reacted with righteous outrage to the Communications Decency Act was generally silent on welfare repeal expected to plunge an additional one million children into poverty.

The maturation of this culture will depend in part on its willingness to recognize that it is a nation only metaphorically. Politics and culture are not one: participating in a culture does not make you part of a political community. Politics comprises political action, not mere cultural affinity. Perhaps netizens will learn this lesson from the censorious Communications Decency Act. Before congratulating themselves on abhorring the CDA and protesting it once it was passed, they might ask themselves where they were when it was drafted and considered by Congress. The American

Civil Liberties Union, which took the lead in challenging the CDA in court, also tried hard to prevent its passage. Politics is action, not attitude. A culture that disdains dealing with politicians leaves itself at their mercy.

Wendy Kaminer
Cambridge, Massachusetts

INDEX

Videotape, effect on campaign
coverage, 25-26
Violence and crime, 100-101
Visual imagery, 26, 28

Walesa, Lech, 68
Walker, Chip, 63
Wal-Mart Corporation, 105, 129-139
Wal-Mart Nation, 113
Washington Post, 35-36
Weather Site (America Online), 27
Web. *See also* Digital culture; Digital
Nation; Internet
chaotic public forums on, 118-119
columns on, 4-6, 126-127
(*See also* Reader response to
Web columnists)
corporate control of, 22, 71-73
hostile communications on, 6-8, 9,
13-17
interactivity on, 4, 8, 10-12
visual nature of, 26

Well, The, 9, 56, 120
White, Otis, 106
Winner, Langdon, 80
Wired (periodical), 46
Wolcott, James, 10-12
Women
media stereotypes of female
athletes, 122-124
mental dialogues of, 75
postings by, 9-10
Woodward, Bob, 73, 74
World Wide Web. *See* Web
Writing, as introspective vs.
collaborative, 140-141

X-Files (television), 101-103

Young adults, 61-63, 99, 124-129